# Nollywood

## The Making of
## a Film Empire

COLUMBIA GLOBAL REPORTS
NEW YORK

# Nollywood
## The Making of
## a Film Empire

# Emily Witt

Niger

Burkina
Faso

Benin

Togo

Niger R.

Nigeria

★ Abuja

Lagos

Asaba

● Warri

Gulf of Guinea

© 2016 Jeffrey L. Ward

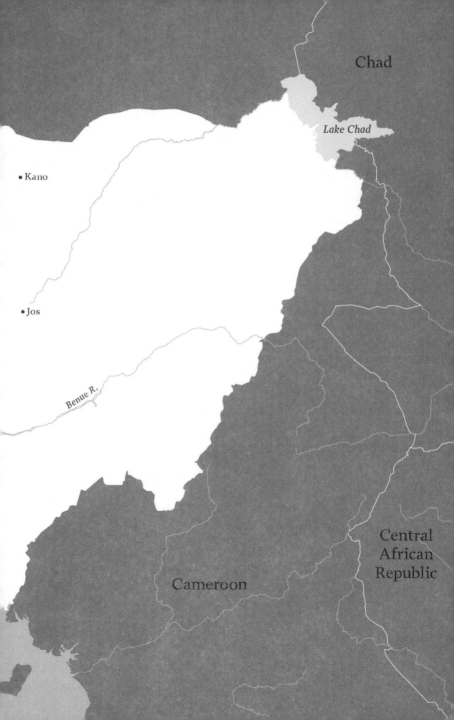

Published by Columbia Global Reports
91 Claremont Avenue, Suite 515
New York, NY 10027
globalreports.columbia.edu
facebook.com/columbiaglobalreports
@columbiaGR

Library of Congress Control Number: 2016962878
ISBN: 978-0997126488

Book design by Strick&Williams
Map design by Jeffrey L. Ward
Author photograph by Noah Kalina

Printed in the United States of America

# CONTENTS

# Prologue

*I had been in Lagos for more than two weeks when, during an inter-*
*view with an executive of a cable company, I mentioned that I still*
*had not found my way onto a Nollywood movie set. She nodded,*
*thought for a moment, then picked up her phone. When someone in*
*Lagos suggests that you should talk to someone else, she will often*
*call that person up then and there. I soon found myself sitting in a bar*
*with Femi Odugbemi, the founder of a documentary festival in Lagos*
*and a producer on a popular soap opera. Odugbemi made some more*
*calls, and by the end of our meeting I had a list of movies in produc-*
*tion. First, however, as an orientation, he gave me a short overview of*
*Nollywood. I decided that what he told me I should simply transcribe*
*here for the reader's benefit:*

Up until the last twenty to thirty years the history and culture
of African communities were the narratives of the colonialists.

Those narratives, quite frankly, beyond not being accurate, beyond not being authentic, were political.

Now: cinema is political. Every cinema is political. The only way cinema works for you is if you are in charge of it. Every colony used cinema—whether in the genre of documentary or the genre of drama—they used cinema to what? To alter behavior. They used cinema to explain that it was civilized to use knives and forks to eat, as though the natives were not eating before they came. There was a replacement therapy and film was the tool. If you knew a god before they came, cinema was able to give you a greater god, and a better god, and explain to you why your god was rubbish. If you dressed a certain way before they came, they were able to use cinema to assure you that what the queen approved as gentlemanly was a suit. Film allowed you to be able to show, to tell, to wow, to entertain—while indoctrinating. Unless you were in control of that, your story was at risk. Your story was told by someone else.

When Nollywood started out in the 1980s, the executive producers were actually merchants who sold videotapes. Someone had the brilliant idea that the way to move these videotapes was to put something on them. Now, at that time, locally produced soap operas were very popular on NTA, the Nigerian Television Authority. And a videotape salesman named Kenneth Nnebue thought to himself, if I could get one of these guys who made the soap opera at NTA to make me something like a soap opera, then we'll move the sales of the tapes. It turned out to be brilliant. But also at that time, like a perfect storm, security was an issue, the military regime was in place, and people wanted to stay at home. The tape players were new, and it was a sign of elitism to be able to watch a film in your own house. The cinemas were going down. We grew up in a time where we could go to cinemas and our mothers didn't care where we were. But cinemas were dying, there was crime in the streets, the military were out there...you know what I mean. So how did the tapes move? The merchants commissioned the soap opera producers: Make me what was essentially an episode, write and direct it for me, and put it on the tape. It moved the tapes. What they didn't sell, they wiped, and made another film.

The way to distribute it was simple: The tapes were simply placed in every electronics shop. It was at that time mostly urban, essentially sold in Lagos. And then, guess what? The house girls and house boys who came from the village and lived with their principals in Lagos found it to be something to watch when madam and *oga* [Yoruba for "sir" or "boss"] were not at home. In that boring period during the day when there was nothing happening, they slotted in the tape. The stories were representations of those things that were present-day realities: big houses, lots of cars, house girls, madam, *oga*. The stories were all about those experiences.

From the 1990s to the 2000s, the industry began to expand. The limits of the experience of the house girl in Lagos were exhausted, but she had a local life in the village. The stories moved to the village; the people who were the consumers began to become the storytellers. And in 1990 to 2000 the whole concept of spiritualism—otherworldliness—emerged. We began to take on the point of view of the house girl, who believed that the unseen controlled the seen. In the village she had mythology, she had *juju* to deal with. You get it? So the stories all became the house girl that brought *juju*, the house girl that took madam's husband.

The way that the movies were distributed also changed. The film left the urban and began to go into the rural areas. The girls, when they go home for their holidays, or to go and see mama that is sick, took along with them videos of Nollywood. By then the story was also now relevant to those down there. They understood the otherwordly thing, they understood all of that. And they embraced it.

By 2000 the VIIS was at the end. The VIIS machine disappeared. Everything became cheaper. There was this video-CD thing, where you could now have one film, two films, three films, in one. VCDs came and they were cheaper. Everybody had the player, including mama in the village, including the grandma, and then the ownership of Nollywood shifted from the makers to the consumers. And that's when a young man who was working with a new cable company decided that, You know what? This is something that needs to be put on cable. Rather than consuming this a little, why don't we make it a twenty-four-hour channel, just place all this junk on it. But you know why he did that? They were cleaning up the tapes from the last film to the next film. In effect, what he did, he became the first archivist.

The archiving turning point brought value to what was before then essentially disposable. By bringing it on TV, he

16    gave it value. In giving it value those people who were wiping
could license content. That's when Nollywood became international. Up until that point it wasn't actually even addressed as
cinema—which is still a matter of debate. But if cinema is about
representation, cultural representation, you have to understand
it is in the present a work of process. Now, 2003, it hit television.
In hitting the TV, roles began to be redefined. By this time the
man that is doing Nollywood just to sell tapes has disappeared.
Why? His reason for being has disappeared. An audience has
taken ownership. A platform has emerged. The sustainability
and longevity of content as something that is valuable enough to
be paid for has emerged. And thus you now have a different mix.

From 2000 to 2010, a few things are beginning to come
together. A star system is emerging; looking for storytelling in a
formal sort of way is emerging; a class of writers and filmmakers
and cameramen. There is a certain consciousness now that what
we are doing actually has a meaning. It was at that same time
that festivals began to be interested in what is this activity in
this Nigeria, and curiosity. Remember, suddenly out of nowhere,
a country is producing dramatic features in the thousands. So it
turns out that academia is interested. Some festivals are interested. Everybody's asking now, What's this activity?

What they discovered, which was quite shocking, was that
it was, how shall I say it? It grew on its own steam. Its origi-
nators were Nigerians, its performers were Nigerians, its audience[s] were Nigerians. Why? They all shared a certain one
common thing: the Nigerian experience.

So the 2000s were the time where we were all seeking an
understanding, both internally and externally, of this thing.
There were a lot of crises in trying to define what it is. The
people who were doing it didn't have the formal education of
film. The people who were doing it were simply expression-
ists, as artists. They were not the highest expression of the
art form. They did not even know what cinema might be, but
they were connecting. They told urban tales people lived and
swore by. And the first thing to grow was not their storytelling
capacity, it was their audience. That really was what made Nollywood unique across the world. The audience grew, before the
birth, before those driving it. The audience embraced it even
before the owners knew what it was. And you know what was
even more interesting? The audience chose it before international foreign stuff. And that's enough for you to understand my
constant conversation about Nollywood being documentary. It
was the answer to colonial narratives.

There were a lot of films in Nigeria through the years, but
none spoke our voice. None recognized our existence as a distinct culture, as a distinct civilization, a distinct aspiration.
We were just defined in one single...you know what they call
poverty porn? The little boy starving with big inflated stomach
defined our narrative. Well guess what? It was from Nollywood
that people first realized that we build houses with huge big
columns and we could afford it. It was from Nollywood that we
first realized that we had people that bought seven, eight cars,
and they only had one wife. It was from Nollywood that you

18    found out that we cheat on our wives too, it's not a privilege of
the West.

It was from Nollywood you knew about the power struc-
tures of our communities, our consideration of spirituality,
a very important component of who we are. Respect for our
elders. The morality of our environment. How we looked at
things like death, things like life. Our respect—all of those
things that basically define who we are began to be evinced with
those films. So whatever its imperfection, Nollywood, in 2000
to 2010, became our voice, and thus our documentary. We did
not need you to create a space for us.

As the star system was built, respect came to the creative
process. In the beginning, those that started were the electronics sellers, the distributors. They called themselves the
marketers. As the years passed they became the producers. They
would give three million *naira* to the boys who went to make the
film. The boys brought the film back, and the marketers sold it.
Every week in the market in Lagos, in Abuja, in Aba, the marketers guaranteed that every Monday new films would come,
and they were all on DVDs.

Now from 2010 to 2015, the landscape has shifted. Suddenly
banks now have film desks. The federal government of Nigeria
suddenly rebases its economy, to admit the number of young
people who are catered for by Nollywood. Suddenly the Bank of
Industry is willing to give money to filmmakers. Suddenly the
federal government, through the Minister of Finance, has given
a fund to train filmmakers, a fund to give to filmmakers, so once
again the funding shifts. It shifts, and formalizes much more.

You're now in 2015. Now you have a multi-fiduciary channel for Nollywood. Today Nollywood is sold in the market, Nollywood has got cinemas, Nollywood is on cable TV, Nollywood is in Netflix. Nollywood is at your beck and call, your arm's reach, via all media regardless of where you are.

One thing has remained the same: the audience of Nollywood has not shifted. The same. Beyond the curious and the academic, there are not many people outside of African experience who have ventured to even understand what Nollywood is trying to do, and I think that's the biggest confirmation of the political nature of cinema. Nollywood has not sought authentication. It has not sought permission to intrude into the cinema space. Its death has been predicted over and over again.

The only reason it has not died is it became owned by the people whose history it was telling.

—Femi Odugbemi, Freedom Park, Lagos,
November 2015

*Living in Bondage* is the story of a man who sacrifices his wife to a satanic cult in exchange for a lifetime of riches. Numbers are difficult to come by in Nollywood but most estimates put sales of the original VHS version in the hundreds of thousands. When I went to Alaba Market the DVD was still available on the shelves of a market stall, twenty-three years after its original release. More importantly, the movie inspired an industry.

*Living in Bondage* begins with the plight of Andy Okeke (Kenneth Okonkwo), a frustrated trader living in Lagos. He is the least successful of his friends, all of whom, complains Andy, "have bought a Mercedes Benz each." Andy is jealous of their success, and spends hours each day lamenting the symbols of their elevated status. "Their houses represent beauty," he says with a sigh. "They are the highest donors at any social gathering."

Andy hungers so much for money that he cannot see the greatest asset in his life: Merit, his patient and loving wife (played by Nnenna Nwabueze-Okonta).

"All the time you torment yourself with negative thoughts about money," she chastises Andy. "Peace and happiness: They're the most important things in life."

But Andy can't stop. He goes out to dinner with his friend Paulo (Okey Ogunjiofor), who has four cars for his personal use ("Mercedes Benz, Rolls Royce, Nissan Patrol, and a Lexus."). He accompanies Paulo to a party, where one businessman "has eight containers coming in weekly, all containing spare auto

parts." The rich friends drink wine, pass around plates heaped
with pieces of chicken, and dance to the music of Jody Watley.

Andy soon learns why they have so much money: They have
each sacrificed the person they love most to the same cult.

"I did it," says one man. "I used my wife. Now I have three
wives. I feed very well; I ride whatever car I choose."

"I did it," says another. "I used my child. Now I ride V-Boot,
ride Pathfinder."

"I used my dear mother. Today I'm money itself."

"I used my dear friend to do it. Today I have many friends.
Courage!"

Paulo, it turns out, got all those cars by sacrificing his sister
to the devil.

At first Andy tries to game the system, bringing in a prostitute for the ritual instead of Merit, but the prostitute invokes
the name of Jesus and flees. Finally he resigns himself to sacrificing Merit. She is drugged and laid out on a table. Her blood is
drawn with a needle and passed around in bowls by the congre-
gants, who sip it with glee. Andy drinks too.

Merit, "so peace-relishing, so respectful, so industrious,
despite her striking beauty" (as one aunt describes her) is now
dead. In the next scene, Andy lives in a mansion filled with
chintz furniture. He has a red Mercedes driven by a chauffeur.
He is finally rich.

"You see you've forgotten your wife now," congratulates
Paulo, when they meet again at a party. "Money is the emperor
of this world." They are discussing the containers of consumer
goods they will import from abroad when the ghost of Merit

22    appears for the first time. She haunts Andy until he again loses
      everything: his job, the Benz, his second wife, and his dignity.

      What made *Living in Bondage* a breakout hit? It was not the
      first VHS movie produced by Kenneth Nnebue, but his ear-
      lier releases were adaptations of Yoruba theater productions.
      Unlike those, *Living in Bondage* represented the life of urban
      Nigerians. It used Igbo as a language not of the ancestral village
      but of the city, of commerce, of modernity. When the movie was
      released with English subtitles, its themes proved just as reso-
      nant to non-Igbo Nigerians. It was a traditional story—about
      Christian morals, marital fidelity, and the hazards of greed—but
      starred recognizable television actors wearing stylish clothes.
      Andy's concerns reflected those of middle-class Nigerians in
      the early 1990s, a time of political instability, inflation, and
      declining per capita income. The characters' obsession with
      containers of imported goods and Japanese cars reflects the ele-
      vated status of those objects following market deregulation, the
      decline of local industry, and the devaluation of the naira. At the
      same time as the Nigerian middle class faced a precarious eco-
      nomic reality, a visible and wealthy elite continued to enjoy the
      profits of the nation's oil revenues. In the movie such wealth is
      viewed with skepticism—as it was in contemporary life at the
      time, when sudden displays of riches fed rumors about fraternal
      organizations and occult practices.

      The unstable economic reality of the early 1990s deter-
      mined the success of *Living in Bondage* in other ways too. In the
      1980s and early 1990s, Nigerians watched pirated VHS tapes
      of foreign movies, but they also watched the output of the

Nigerian Television Authority, the country's state-owned broad-    23
caster. Even after the network lost its government funding after
structural economic adjustment, corporate brands continued to
sponsor the production of popular soap operas such as Zeb Ejiro's *Ripples*, Amaka Igwe's *Checkmate*, Lola Fani-Kayode's *Mirror
in the Sun*, and comedies like Ken Saro-Wiwa's *Basi and Company*.
By the 1990s these experienced Nigerian television producers
had work, a broadcast outlet, and huge audiences, but not a stable
living—they had to cobble together the funding to buy their own
airtime, and earned no profit commensurate to the sizes of their
audiences. (Anybody could buy airtime on the NTA in the late
1980s and 1990s, which meant that the airwaves often showed
videos of the lavish birthday parties, weddings, and funerals of
the Nigerian elite.) When the success of *Living in Bondage* indicated to television producers that they could directly profit from
their audience via sales of videotapes, they teamed up with marketers and began producing movies independently instead of for
television. *Living in Bondage* established a tone, and an industry,
which soon expanded from its video origins to the cinema, satellite television, and the screens of mobile phones, and from the
confines of Nigeria to the rest of the continent and the world.

# A Premiere

The first of what real-estate developers call "international-standard" malls to open in Lagos was The Palms, which was completed in 2005 in the neighborhood of Lekki. The Palms was low-slung and white, smallish by American standards of shopping centers, with an anemic selection of the eponymous palms placed in planters around the parking lot. Security guards checked trunks before letting cars into the lot and purses before letting shoppers through the sliding doors. The mall's anchor tenants were the South African supermarket chain Shoprite and the South African superstore Game. The Palms also had a Cold Stone Creamery ice cream shop, a branch of the woman's clothing chain Mango, and a pharmacy where foreigners could buy their malaria prophylaxis in counterfeit-proof packaging with hologram stickers. The electricity was steady here, the climate controlled. The tiled floors shone. Outside was the informal economy: hawkers selling gasoline from jerry cans,

windshield wiper blades, shrimp crackers, and newspapers
to people in traffic jams. Inside the prices were fixed, the pace
unhurried, the aisles uncrowded. While I once saw a shouting
match happen over the cash registers at Game, the cause of which
I failed to discern, for the most part nobody shouted at each other
at The Palms. The shelves of Shoprite gleamed with the inter-
nationally branded cookies and breakfast cereals that no one in
Nigeria seemed to eat. The escalators rolled in seamless motion.

Like most malls, The Palms had a multiplex. The Genesis
Deluxe Cinema screened the latest Nigerian movies alongside
the most recent chapters of *James Bond*, *Star Wars*, and *X-Men*.
On weekend nights, it was also a preferred venue for red carpet
premieres of Nigerian movies. These pageants happened on a
near-weekly basis, celebrations for the highest-budget productions, the ones with the biggest stars. On my second night
in Lagos, I ascended the escalators of The Palms to attend the
premiere of *Road to Yesterday,* a new drama starring Genevieve
Nnaji.

I had been advised, in advance, to bring high heels to Lagos,
a city where tailors sew bespoke formalwear for the rich and the
poor alike and where the latest trends in globalized fast fashion
are recreated in wax-print textiles for the wealthy patrons of
the nightclubs of Lagos. As in Milan or Paris, to attend a party
in Lagos looking ordinary or mass-produced was seen as an
affront, a wasted opportunity to bring joy via carefully selected
adornment. For the premiere, the mall multiplex had been
transformed with a red carpet, a photography scrum, and the
lavish plumage of the Nollywood elite: Rita Dominic in a jaunty

26   black pantsuit with rhinestone-studded heels; Funke Akindele in a short-sleeved red dress draped with golden spangles; Desmond Elliot in a blue dinner jacket with a pink silk handkerchief; Ramsey Nouah in a leather newsboy cap, a linen scarf, and blue jeans. The premiere's attendees posed for photographs and ate canapés, adorned with paisley pocket squares, peplums, gold lamé, satin trains, high-waisted silk pajamas, fedoras, clear plastic Oxford shoes, Nehru collars, a red velvet smoking jacket. A woman in a white shorts suit patterned with birds of paradise laughed with another whose stilettos tapered into monarch butterflies at the ankles. One up-and-coming starlet wore an off-the-shoulder dress of black shag like the fur of a Newfoundland dog, which kept catching on the buttons of people brushing past her. Genevieve Nnaji was a vision of purity, graceful in a floor-length white dress with billowy sleeves. Now in her late thirties, she had a regal bearing and a steady gaze, a tall, doe-eyed beauty whose shyness was tempered by a hint of aloofness. She posed for pictures, her face fixed in a slight, effortless smile.

Oprah Winfrey once called Genevieve Nnaji "the Julia Roberts of Africa," but the comparison does not suffice. The industry of Nollywood and the career of Genevieve Nnaji emerged almost simultaneously; she is its Julia Roberts and its Audrey Hepburn. When the matatu driver of Nairobi or the kelewele vendor of Accra or the bartender in a shebeen in Soweto think of Nigeria, they will likely think of Genevieve, the former face of Lux soap in Africa, a brand ambassador of Range Rover, the star of over eighty Nollywood movies. Nnaji has 2.9 million followers on Instagram. She has a white bichon-frise named

Prince. She is unmarried but had a daughter as a teenager, a sensitive story she discusses only obliquely when she recounts her middle-class Igbo-Catholic upbringing in Lagos ("Everybody falls," she said in one interview I saw. "That's what makes us human.") Her online fans refer to themselves as "Genevites" and leave their comments with the hashtag #Slaynevieve. Below YouTube videos of her work are comments that proclaim Nnaji a luminary not only to Nigerians but to the continent at large. "Nnaji is Queen!! Damn!! Her carriage is everything. Am so proud to be a Nigerian," they write. "I love u so much Queen Genevieve. U are the pride of Africa, a Super Shining Star."

Nnaji was born on May 3, 1979—a Taurus, as she likes to remind her followers on social media. She began acting at the age of eight, on the Nigerian Television Authority soap opera *Ripples*. The show ended in 1993, when its creator, Zeb Ejiro, joined the exodus of local television producers who had started making straight-to-video movies and distributing them in the physical marketplace rather than over the airwaves. Nnaji followed many other television actors into the video movie industry. She starred in her first Nollywood movie, *Most Wanted*, in 1998, at the age of nineteen.

Her fame grew with such hits as *Sharon Stone* (2002), a morality tale in which Nnaji, as Sharon Stone, uses wealthy men as her sexual pawns. "I've decided to pay men back in their own coin," she says, after sleeping with three of them in a single day. Things don't end well for Sharon Stone. The men discover they've been used, and conspire to trick her in return. One man proposes marriage, than fails to show up to the wedding. "Lagos

28    traffic?" suggests an optimistic marriage registrar as Sharon
      Stone realizes she has been jilted. The abandoned bride drives
      the wedding car to the groom's house, balloons flying, where she
      finds him playing checkers and drinking beer with the other two
      men. They make a sarcastic toast to the bride. She faints to the
      floor in her white gown. Fade to black.

      Nnaji no longer makes movies like *Sharon Stone, Sharon
      Stone 2,* or *Sharon Stone in Abuja.* Also in her past are *Blood Sister*
      (2003), about a jealous sibling feud, or *Above Death* (2003),
      where a woman is raped by an evil entity and conceives a cursed
      child, or *He Lives In Me* (2004), where Nnaji's character is visited
      by a ghost who has come back from the dead to prevent her from
      falling in love with a murderer, or *Games Women Play* (2005),
      where her character dispatches her best friend to seduce her
      fiancé as a test of his loyalty. Nnaji has stopped making the low-
      budget, straight-to-video melodramas that built her career, in
      part because the industry changed.

      When Nnaji began acting in movies in the late 1990s, the
      spontaneous and accelerated growth of Nollywood was hap-
      pening in a country with virtually no movie screens. For its
      first few years of existence, even The Palms had no movie the-
      ater. Lagos is a city of 21 million people that as recently as
      2004 had no cinemas at all. This wasn't always the case. Lago-
      sians who grew up in the city in the 1950s and 60s will rem-
      inisce about watching *Lawrence of Arabia, Sinbad the Sailor,*
      Hollywood westerns, and Bollywood musicals in neighborhood
      movie theaters. After independence in 1960, Nigerians started
      making their own celluloid films, classics like *Kongi's Harvest*

(a 1970 adaptation of Wole Soyinka's play). Nigerian directors such as Hubert Ogunde, Jab Adu, Ola Balogun, Adeyemi Afolayan (known as Ade Love), and Eddie Ugbomah made popular movies, some of them drawing on the narratives of traditional Yoruba and Igbo theater, some of them telling more contemporary stories.

This cinema culture collapsed in the 1980s. Some people claimed the problem began as far back as 1972, when General Yakubu Gowon issued an "indigenization decree" which nationalized foreign-owned businesses—including cinemas, many of which were owned by Lebanese immigrants. Others blamed the structural economic adjustment program imposed on Nigeria by the International Monetary Fund in 1986, which devalued the local currency and made it difficult to import goods, including films and film stock. Another explanation was a perceived decline in security around the same time. Middle class city dwellers did not want to get robbed, so they stayed home and watched movies on VCRs instead. There was, then and now, the difficulty of ensuring a steady supply of electricity, and the cost of running a generator. The movie halls were converted to make way for a new pastime, Pentecostal Christianity. By end of the 1980s, Nigeria's cinemas had mostly disappeared.

It was in part the decline of Nigerian cinema that precipitated the rise of what we know today as Nollywood, which grew out of the demand from this stay-at-home, VHS-watching audience. Cinema in Lagos reappeared in the new century, with the country's return to democracy in 1999, with its economic revival, with security improved, and with the construction of

30    malls, but it took years before the industry that was churning out thousands of movies on discs started releasing them on the big screen.

The first multiplex cinema in Nigeria was the Silverbird Galleria on Victoria Island, which opened in 2004. The founder was a businessman named Ben Murray-Bruce, who earned his undergraduate degree in marketing from the University of South Carolina and who has since become a senator of the republic.

Murray-Bruce thought that if there could be movie theaters in Shanghai or Johannesburg there could be movie theaters in Lagos. It took him ten years to convince the banks that if they financed a theater, the people would come. The first feature to show at the first multiplex in Nigeria was Mel Gibson's *Passion of the Christ*. So eager were Lagosians to watch Jesus being flayed with barbed whips on the big screen that the people of Lagos gave the movie its highest grossing opening weekend in Africa.

The Palms got its multiplex in 2008. At first the Genesis Deluxe, like the Silverbird, showed only foreign films, mostly from Hollywood. The local theater chains began screening Nigerian movies only in 2009 (or at least screening them the normal way—producers could rent screens for private parties and premieres from the outset). The argument against screening Nigerian movies commercially was that nobody would pay 1,500 naira (about $7.50 in 2015) to watch something they could buy on the street on a disc for a tenth of the price, especially if the sound warbled in and out and production values looked like those of a used car salesman's ad on late-night television in Milwaukee. The format of early Nollywood movies fell somewhere between a soap opera and a feature film. Because they were meant to be watched on a television rather than in a movie theater, the production values didn't need to be high, and standardized movie conventions were ignored. One movie might be four hours long, divided into two or three chapters that were sold first as separate tapes and later as discs.

Things have changed: Ben Murray-Bruce said that he now considered the future of the Nigerian multiplex to be in Nollywood movies, not Hollywood. The cinema-going audience is still only a fraction of the Nigerian population, but in a country of 180 million people a fraction is significant. In Lagos, going to the movies has become a good way for middle-class professionals working on the islands to wait out the traffic to the mainland at the end of the day, when endless lines of trucks and buses inch across the Third Mainland Bridge. On the mainland, at the Ikeja City Mall, the theaters are packed on weekends, and in recent years a new chain, Film House, has been experimenting with offering a more affordable cinematic experience, with tickets for 500 naira in the mainland neighborhood of Surulere, a third of the going price in the wealthier enclaves of Lagos.

Running a multiplex in Nigeria comes with a unique set of challenges. The night of the *Road to Yesterday* premiere, I was introduced to the chief executive director of Film House, an enthusiastic thirty-two-year-old in a tuxedo named Moses Babatope. Babatope said his company, which now has eleven multiplexes in Nigeria, must fend off competition from pirates and deal with infrastructural shortcomings like unreliable

32 public transportation and constant power outages. He has also confronted the managerial problems of training staff in a country where many young adults have no experience with cinema culture. Like many Nigerian entrepreneurs, Babatope and Film House's CEO Kene Mkparu are dual citizens of the United Kingdom. Both returned to Nigeria after working for the Odeon cinema chain in England with the hopes of exploiting what Babatope called "virgin terrain."

"It's a population of 180 million-plus people, there are less than 20 cinemas, less than 120 screens, for people that churn out two [or] three thousand titles a year," Babatope said. "I thought it was too compelling not to come here, to try and grow it, to double the number and even beyond that." The numbers are still small, but growth has been steady, with 2016 breaking all previous box office records for Nigerian cinema movies, and nearly 30 percent of the $11.5 million box office total coming from local movies. (The highest grossing Nigerian movie at the cinema to date is a 2016 release called *The Wedding Party*, a comedy that celebrates and lampoons Nigeria's great tradition of ostentatious weddings. It earned $1.4 million at the box office, a record for a Nigerian movie, but since the movie was also pirated and distributed on DVD and online, its total financial earnings are difficult to quantify.)

The rise of the multiplex in Nigeria also encouraged the improvement in Nollywood production values. The cameras have gone high-definition, the boom mike is less likely to creep into the frame, and the editors no longer include two-minute shots of people exiting Toyota Camrys and walking uneventfully into houses. To differentiate the better-produced, made-for-cinema movies from their VHS predecessors, these movies are often referred to as the "New Nollywood." Because such movies are also sometimes made by foreign-educated young people from Nigeria's economic elite—a relatively new trend—there is occasionally talk of a "gentrification" of Nollywood. As actors such as Genevieve Nnaji have pursued bigger-budget movies with cinema releases, one prominent Nollywood director accused her and other actors of "biting the fingers" that fed them.

The New Nollywood movies aspire, like the malls in which they are screened, to be "international-standard," to rank alongside Hollywood, Bollywood, and the soap operas of Latin America or Korea in networks of global distribution and international audiences. They tend to clock closer to the standard ninety minutes in length, and their plots tend to be less sprawling than the old Nollywood movies. But it is the lower budget movies, with their folklore and their flaws, that earned the affection of African audiences in the first place, and these older format movies are still produced by the hundreds each year. However one chooses to characterize the schism, there is a recognizable divide between the movies on sale five to a video CD in the great markets of Lagos and those that play to a wealthier audience in the cinema, a divide enhanced by the class hierarchy of one of the most economically unequal societies in the world.

*

34     *Road to Yesterday* was Nnaji's first leading role since the criti-
       cally panned 2013 adaptation of Chimamanda Ngozi Adichie's
       Biafran War novel *Half a Yellow Sun*, and also Nnaji's first ven-
       ture as a producer. She wrote the story on which the screen-
       play was based. Her co-producers, Chinny Onwugbenu and
       ChiChi Nwoko, are businesswomen around Nnaji's age who
       both attended university in the United States but have focused
       their investments in Africa: Onwugbenu started a makeup com-
       pany, and Nwoko expanded the *American Idol* franchise to Nige-
       rian television. The screenwriter and director, Ishaya Bako, was
       born in 1986 and attended film school in London.

       We filed into the screening rooms. The director's grandfa-
       ther, who wore a green sport coat, a yellow shirt, and a base-
       ball cap, took pictures of the audience on his tablet computer.
       The leading lady was hailed as "a woman that needs no intro-
       duction, the quintessential screen goddess: Genevieve Nnaji."
       Nnaji serenely acknowledged the applause.

       Eating popcorn from specially printed *Road to Yesterday*
       boxes and drinking Fantas and Sprites, we settled in to watch
       the movie. *Road to Yesterday* begins with a plane landing on the
       tarmac at Murtala Mohammed Airport in Lagos. Victoria (Nnaji)
       has returned to Nigeria from London to attend the funeral of an
       uncle and confront the ruins of her marriage. She arrives home
       to Izu (Oris Erhuero), her estranged husband. The scene is bleak:
       The shades of their home are drawn; Izu is sprawled in front of
       a table filled with empty bottles and glasses. They spend the
       night avoiding each other, then get in their Land Rover to travel
       to the funeral.

Trapped in a car for many hours, they confront the history of their relationship. It is a story told in flashbacks: the instantaneous connection of their first meeting, the infidelities committed by both, the paternity crisis that ultimately divided them (their daughter has sickle cell anemia, but Izu had tested negative for the gene). They argue, they cajole, they berate, they apologize, but eventually they reconcile in a boutique hotel.

Except . . . it was all a dream! Victoria suddenly awakes at Izu's bedside. He is in the hospital, attached to a beeping heart monitor, mangled from a car accident that happened the night of her arrival. The road to yesterday happened only in Victoria's imagination. It is too late for apologies, for explanations, for forgiveness. The monitor redlines and Izu is dead.

"Why do we love?" asks Victoria in a somber voiceover in the last scene, as Izu's coffin is lowered into the ground. "Is it our search for a deeper connection, or are we just afraid of being alone?"

*Road to Yesterday* happens in a very particular Nigeria, in the creamy leather interior of a Land Rover as glossy as a seal just out of the water, in the spacious halls of a mansion where a child's bedroom is a carefully manicured landscape in pink. It is a Nigeria of wealthy couples with repressed emotions, of nannies sweeping children from the room when arguments begin, of helicopter shots of a luxury car speeding down an unimpeded highway. The vision of spare elegance breaks only once, when the couple stops for lunch at the fast-food chain Chicken Republic and a few street vendors can be seen out of focus in the background, milling around outside.

36    But it's movieland, not Nigeria, and nobody cares if the Lagos of movieland is only a sterile facsimile of the chaotic Lagos of real life. The only complaint I heard, regarding the movie's authenticity, was that funerals in Nigeria were not mafialike affairs of dark sunglasses or black suits, of tears rolling silently down cheeks. At Nigerian funerals, I was assured, the mourners wail, they scream, they try to throw themselves into the grave.

At the premiere, the audience laughed in recognition when Victoria and Izu got pulled over at a police checkpoint, and whistled when Izu lied about his extramarital affair. "I have no evil intentions toward you," said Izu, on screen. "So they always say Papa!" heckled a member of the audience. And then, when the couple finally reconciled, in a steamy shower scene, "Please don't make no cut!" When the plot twist of Izu's untimely death was revealed, Chioma "Chigul" Omeruah, a comedian sitting next to me who played Victoria's jolly best friend, wiped away genuine tears.

The after party was held at a restaurant in Victoria Island called The Foundry. We sat in the humid night in white-curtained cabanas around a pool that had inflatable beach balls and water guns floating in it. My gin and tonic came with a curly straw, colored lights moved to the rhythm of an auto-tuned Nigerian pop song, and waiters circulated with dishes of prawns, fish, and French fries. I chatted with a Korean American couple who lived and worked in Lagos, friends of one of the producers. We talked about how the future of self-driving

cars might one day improve the traffic here. They had recently
tried to cut back on drinking to try and lose weight. They told
me about their weekend jet ski excursions, which they organized with friends, zooming eight miles out into the ocean to
commune with migratory pods of humpback whales, accompanied by two rescue boats. "There aren't any rules here," the
woman said with a shrug.

Amaka Igwe was another transplant from the Nigerian Television Authority who became a Nollywood pioneer. Igwe died of an asthma attack in 2014 at the age of fifty-one after a successful career in radio and television, but it was her movies from the 1990s that made her famous. A former soap-opera director, Igwe helped establish the hybrid movie-length soap operas that became characteristic of Nollywood of the era.

Among her greatest hits was *Violated*, which tells the story of Peggy (Ego Boyo), a woman from a poor rural background who has moved to the city and is working at a supermarket when she falls in love with Tega (Richard Mofe-Damijo), a wealthy businessman whose mother, a super-snob played by Joke Silva, does not approve of the match.

The scheming gold digger who tries to steal a wealthy man's money is a common plot in Nollywood morality tales. Here Peggy distinguishes herself by earning her own income and contributing to the household even after she marries Tega. Her financial and spiritual independence prevent her from falling prey to the schemes of her mother-in-law, who tries to pay her to disappear. But Peggy has her own dark past, a secret she left behind in the village that carries over into her new life as a power suit—wearing bourgeois.

In a stratified society, Peggy crosses lines, equally fluent when yelling at a villain in pidgin as when she is ordering a

dinner in a fancy Italian restaurant. Her ascension from des-
perate teenage orphan to successful urban bank employee was
accomplished not via black magic but tenacity and hard work.

What sets *Violated* apart is its story structure, which has
more in common with a Latin American telenovela than with a
Hollywood movie. As in a telenovela, multiple storylines begin
independently, becoming increasingly entwined as backstories
are revealed and ultimately reaching resolution when each character has finally learned all the relevant truths about the others.
Unlike the typical telenovela, which would inch forward across
120 hour-long episodes, the complex plotlines of *Violated* parts
1 and 2 had to be compressed into a mere three hours. Nollywood
still favors this device of parallel but interconnected storylines,
their plots as minutely detailed as serial television, crammed
into the vessel of feature-length filmmaking.

# A Visit to a Set in Jos

The city of Jos is located in Plateau State, at an elevation of just over 4,000 feet. Stepping off the plane from Lagos onto the tarmac of the small airport in Jos was like taking off a pair of damp socks. The air here was clear and cool. Hills and rock formations punctuated the landscape, which was dotted with herds of white cows, cattle egrets, and goats. The light was golden in the late afternoon, the dirt reddish brown.

I traveled to Jos to meet Okey Ogunjiofor, the actor who had played the character of Paulo in *Living in Bondage* more than two decades before, and had also co-written and helped produce the movie. Now, after a long hiatus from the industry, he was producing his first movie in years.

Financed with a loan from a government fund set up to nurture Nollywood, the movie was a biopic about Queen Amina, a storied warrior princess who ruled what is now Northern Nigeria in the sixteenth century. The movie's director, Izu

Ojukwu, was one of the most promising names of the new generation of movie directors, and he was shooting with a high-end digital camera. If successful, *Queen Amina* could represent a bridge across generations, a connection between the low-budget video movie that birthed the industry and the cinematic potential of the present.

A member of the crew met me at the airport. We drove along highways that were empty compared to the gridlock of Lagos. Along the way we picked up the set's horse trainer, who had been stranded by the side of the road in a three-wheeled *keke* with a flat tire. Then we drove on a ring road on the outskirts of Jos, pulling off eventually on a dirt road surrounded by irrigated tomato farms and dried-up stalks of corn and sorghum.

Being a historical epic, the sets of Queen Amina had to be in places with no traces of modernity, in this case a scenic cow pasture. Evening was not far off when we arrived, and the crew was scrambling to finish shooting a scene before nightfall. I was quickly introduced to the producer and director, then given a Styrofoam container of okra stew, a plastic bottle of water, and a chair next to Ojukwu, the director, who was watching the scene on a monitor. Ojukwu was a calm man with an aversion to raising his voice. It helped, under the circumstances, to be a calm person.

They were shooting a death scene. Before us one of Queen Amina's many lovers was laid out on a pallet made of wood beneath a small, desiccated tree. Amina was to approach his deathbed flanked by her troops, including her personal bodyguard, a wild-looking Amazonian figure who wore a leopard

42    pelt over her shoulders and her hair in a Mohawk. Ojukwu was ordering the ranks of soldiers carrying shields, spears, and flags to disperse more widely across the field.

Amina approached the corpse and delivered her lines.

"He died like a hero," she said, dropping to her knees to embrace his corpse. "He sacrificed his soul to save my life."

She stopped. The script called for the dead lover's necklace to be yanked off, but the necklace wasn't there. Members of the props team began rushing around. Ojukwu looked up from his seat before the monitor in disbelief. "We have less than thirty minutes of light and now a necklace will hold us ransom?"

The assistant director, who was issuing orders through a loudspeaker, apologized to the troops, who were getting restless.

"I'm sorry, I see the ants are stressing you guys," he said. The soldiers appeared to be on the verge of mutiny. "I need water!" pleaded one.

They set up another shot.

"Your cousin will be avenged," Amina said to another character, an estranged childhood playmate.

The soundman, a German named Peter, ripped off his headphones and looked around, glaring. "It sounds like a discotheque," he said.

Through his loudspeaker, the assistant director called for silence. The soundman took a reading then shook his head again.

"Babies," he said.

Some locals who had come to sell sugar cane and watch the shoot under a nearby tree were asked to silence their children.

"Action!" said Ojukwu.

"He died like a hero—" started Amina.

A cell phone rang.

A collective groan went up.

"Drinks on him tonight," said Peter.

The assistant director spoke into his megaphone: "Please, crew members remember to turn off your cell phones and call your mothers and fathers."

Another take.

"He died like a hero—"

"Ali, you're breathing!" yelled the director to Ali Nuhu, a megastar of Nollywood's Hausa-language industry who was supposed to be dead on the pallet.

But finally the scene was done. The golden necklace, which was found after a twenty-minute search, was ripped from the dead man's neck. In the last rays of the setting sun, the amassed troops received their heartbroken warrior queen. Then the light was gone and it was a wrap.

We drove back to Jos in a caravan. We passed a floodlit preacher delivering an outdoor sermon to an audience seated in plastic chairs, shouting to be heard over the generator. We stopped at a police checkpoint on the outskirts of town. They waved us through after checking the trunk. We drove through obscured streets, shadows walking on the sidewalks, the darkness broken only by kerosene lanterns and the occasional generator-powered storefront. The electricity was out and the streets of Jos were very dark.

*

The following day was a day off from shooting, when Ogun-jiofor, Ojukwu, and their crew would recuperate and plan the production schedule for the weeks to come. In the meantime, I toured the production's headquarters with Ogunjiofor.

The cast and crew had taken over the Hill Station Hotel, a decaying grand hotel whose colonial legacy was apparent in its name. The Hill Station was a famous place—the actor Pierce Brosnan, the British prime minister John Major, and the Queen of England all stayed there. Now its swimming pool was empty and cracked, and when the first members of the film crew had arrived two months before the lawns were overgrown with weeds.

The film crew's extended presence had occasioned some-thing of a revival. The grass had been mown and repairs had been made to the rooms, which were themed different colors ranging from baby blue to butter yellow. My own room was orange, with green polka dotted sheets, and a polyester fur blanket showing a peacock in full plumage under an orange bedspread marked with cigarette burns. The bathroom had no toilet seat or show-erhead, and I bathed using a bucket, but the hot water heater worked. At night the generators outside idled like truck engines and I would fall asleep under the slightly menacing gaze of a portrait of a toucan hung on one wall. These were the conditions in which everyone stayed, from Ogunjiofor on down. Nobody complained. The hotel's restaurant appeared not to have served anyone for several years, as I discovered when I tried to get a Nescafé there one morning. The movie crew's food—traditional

Nigerian dishes of stews with pounded yam or rice three times     45
a day—was delivered to them in Styrofoam containers from a
catering company which was, Ojukwu told me, "cutting our
throats." One advantage of the hotel was that it was located next
to an army base, which meant that the film crew had an armed
entourage at night. Jos had been bombed by Boko Haram a few
months before, and signs that the city was in a state of lockdown
ranged from the police checkpoints at its outskirts to the con-
fusion of Sundays, when the roads around the biggest churches
were closed for security.

The evidence of what a single major movie production
could do for the local economy, and how much that economy
benefited from a veritable invasion of dozens of people who
needed food, shelter, drivers, and carpenters, was obvious.
Jos had once been a tourist town known for its temperate climate and pretty landscapes, but the violence of recent years
had decimated that economy. In five weeks in Nigeria I never
saw a tourist. As Chinua Achebe once wrote, "Only a masochist
with an exuberant taste for self-violence will pick Nigeria for a
holiday." The foreigners I did meet in Nigeria were there to do
research for their PhDs or drill for oil or they worked for foreign
governments or they were journalists.

As part of its touristic legacy Jos had a wildlife park, which
was said to be more of a depressing kind of zoo, and while I
was there its sole lion escaped and was shot. I followed the
national newspaper coverage in the days that followed, where
officers responded to queries about the lion's fate with state-
ments such as, "We are somewhere, cannot talk to anyone." This

46    evasion caused lively debate, with readers writing comments like "This is wickedness to a poor, old, harmless cat," and "I am disappointed that the so called joint task force do not have tranquilizers or tasers to use on the Lion than to kill it." They also questioned the keepers' claims that the lion was forty-three years old, as one reader objected, "a Lion cannot live more than twenty years in a cage."

At the time I met Ogunjiofor, I had not yet watched *Living in Bondage*. "I was dashing," said Ogunjiofor, smiling. "You'll love me! You'll wish I wasn't married when you watch it."

I met with him in his suite of rooms at the Hill Station, which were powder blue. He was slight and spry, with sharp features. He was a charismatic storyteller and an unfailing optimist, despite all the obstacles and inconveniences of shooting movies in Nigeria. Since Ojukwu, *Queen Amina*'s director, was a more taciturn and soft-spoken figure, it was Ogunjiofor's energy that carried the production. He had a streak of Puritanism to him that his crew found amusing. He would often refuse food ("I don't want to age so fast," he said. "Food ages. The more you eat the more you age") and would complain when the production left their locations strewn with the plastic bags that had held their water and the pastel-colored Styrofoam containers from their lunches. He made a point of walking (or "trekking," as Nigerians say) to locations to show he did not put on airs. In a country where severity is often expected of people in positions of authority, Ogunjiofor was a shrewd and kindly figure. "What's wrong with you?" he would demand to anyone who looked a little morose, eliciting a smile, or an ashamed confession about a headache. He was a man of faith, and had allied himself with a megachurch and a celebrity preacher. ("Pastor Tunde Bakare. Google him. He's an enigma. Some say he's controversial.")

Now in his early fifties, Ogunjiofor had graduated from the College of Television in Jos in 1987. He left university with a record of good grades and a letter of recommendation to the national broadcaster, the Nigerian Television Authority, but the late 1980s were not a time of abundance in Nigeria, especially not for an aspiring television producer. Equipment was scarce and funding for television stations had withered to almost nothing. When Ogunjiofor showed up at the NTA with his letter, he was told there was an embargo on hiring, but a director took pity and helped him get a job as a video producer for a Nigerian wrestler named Power Mike. Power Mike (his real name was Michael Okpala) was a retired heavyweight champion with a touring wrestling show similar to the WWE. When Power Mike decided to retire, return to his village, and open a gym, Ogunjiofor stayed in Lagos. From 1988 to 1992 he worked as a street hawker, selling women's beauty products.

But he had an idea. He was an Igbo, he said, an ethnic group that is known as "the entrepreneurs of the country, the entrepreneurs of the world, the risk takers." (During the Biafran War, when an attempted secession by the Igbo-dominated eastern half of the country resulted in one million deaths in the late 1960s, the Nigerian government maligned the Igbo as a socially privileged group. Their characterization as a high-achieving minority, along with their persecution on ethnic grounds, led

48     to Biafra-era news articles referring to them as "the Jews of
       West Africa.") Ogunjiofor had noticed that many Igbos owned
       VCRs, on which they watched cassettes of pirated foreign films.
       One day it occurred to him that he could use the electronic
       news-gathering cameras with which he had been trained in tele-
       vision school to tell a fictional story in Igbo that would appeal
       more directly to the VCR owners of Nigeria.

       But he didn't have the camera, or the 150,000 naira he
       estimated he needed to make the movie. Then a friend at the
       National Theater referred Ogunjiofor to a man who imported
       video cassettes from abroad and sold them with pirated foreign
       movies on them. His name was Kenneth Nnebue.

       Nnebue is generally credited as being the father of Nol-
       lywood movies. He began shooting Yoruba-language theater
       productions onto video in the late 1980s. Nnebue's name is in
       the credits for *Living in Bondage* but Ogunjiofor claims the idea
       for the story was originally his. The director was Chris Obi-
       Rapu, who was under an exclusive contract at the NTA at the
       time and therefore is credited as Vic Mordi. (Mordi was his
       wife's maiden name.)

       Ogunjiofor, Obi-Rapu, and Nnebue have each been credited
       with the success of *Living in Bondage*, but the truth seems to be
       that it was a collaborative effort. I called Nnebue several times
       to hear his take but he told me he no longer discusses Nolly-
       wood, a chapter of a past that he renounced after finding Jesus.
       He hasn't left the business completely. The Facebook page of
       Brother Kenneth Nnebue Film Evangelism invites viewers to
       share the "GOOD NEWS!": "unlimited films that will not only

touch your soul but will soak you in the living water of the spirit
of God where you will hunger and thirst no more, where your
never ending questions will be answered, and spiritual mys-
teries will be revealed unto you." In 2015 Nnebue sold the rights
to *Living in Bondage* for an English-language remake featuring
Nollywood megastar Ramsey Nouah.

"This storytelling quality of Africans is huge," said Ogunjiofor, after reminiscing about the movie's success. "Everything is storytelling. We are all storytellers. And the stories are
amazing. That's one. Two: We celebrate family values, which is
no longer available out there. Family values is what Africans are
known for: morals, things that ordinarily someone would see
outside and say 'it's forbidden.'"

He compared a Nigerian movie to a Hollywood block-
buster, "which starts with destruction and ends with destruction. It's nothing. Voom-voom-voom—effects! Rah rah rah,
bring things down and bring them up again. Blah blah blah,
aliens are fighting and eating rubbish. What do you learn from
it? Just that it was able to hold you and you're watching like
this? And then you say 'what happened?' Nothing. Here you
get a moral, something touches your soul, something touches
your spirit, it's like preaching a message," he said. "We celebrate those things: family values, communal living, and then
our lifestyles, our hairdos, and all these things, we are really
into them and we want to see them."

After *Living in Bondage*, Ogunjiofor made other movies,
some of them huge hits: *Ashes of Hatred, Nneka the Pretty Serpent, Brotherhood of Darkness, When Flowers Turn Black*. But

50    Nollywood changed. In the mid-1990s it was ruled, said Ogun-
      jiofor, by the experienced NTA producers, who had some com-
      mitment to quality.

          This promising phase only lasted until 1998. The mar-
      keters, who copied and distributed the VHS tapes to the streets,
      decided to try and cut out the middlemen and make movies
      themselves, or to hire the cheapest directors they could. The
      quality of the movies declined. But now, with the return of cin-
      emas, Ogunjiofor saw the whole industry being uplifted again.

          "We're going to churn out movies in Nigeria, by Nige-
      rians, but for the world. And then Nigerian films, called Nolly-
      wood, will take the stage globally," said Ogunjiofor who had just
      refused his lunch. "Look where we have gone, with the trash we
      are producing! When big money comes here, the type of talent,
      the type of environment that we have, the beautiful sceneries
      everywhere, the topography, the creative ingenuity, and the
      pleasure we take to do so much with little is here." He laughed.
      "So," he said. "That is why you are here."

      When Ogunjiofor went to examine the historic record for the
      biography of Queen Amina of Zazzau he found her reputation to
      be corrupted. Ogunjiofor wanted to make a movie about female
      empowerment, and he dedicated it to the girls who were kid-
      napped by the terrorist group Boko Haram from the northern
      Nigerian village of Chibok in 2014. The 276 girls, most of them
      Christians, were taken from their boarding school by Islamist
      militants. A global "Bring Back Our Girls" campaign emerged
      on social media in the months following the mass abduction,

but it was not until 2017 that the first negotiated exchange released around 100 of the abducted girls. The kidnappings not only brought attention to the ongoing conflict in Northern Nigeria, but also prompted a discussion in the country about women's rights. Ogunjiofor wanted to install Queen Amina in the pantheon of mythic female Africans, allow her to assume her rightful place alongside the Queen of Sheba from Ethiopia, Cleopatra and Nefertiti of Egypt, and Queen Nzinga of Angola. He also wanted to make a movie that broke down the division between Nigeria's mostly Muslim north and its Christian south. The cultural division is reflected in Nollywood too, with movies made in its Hausa-language northern epicenter, Kano, rarely finding audiences in the south and east of the country, and vice versa.

Amina inherited the throne from her father in sixteenth-century Nigeria. "If you read her history on the Internet she's painted as a wicked woman who doesn't like men, who sleeps with them and kills them in the morning because she doesn't want anyone to see her nakedness," said Ogunjiofor. When I looked it up I discovered this was true. One website described her as taking "a temporary husband from the legions of vanquished foes after every battle," like Genghis Khan. Ogunjiofor offered a revisionist history of Amina's romantic problems: She had been surrounded by plotting usurpers who planted rivals as her suitors. "So no matter how ferociously Amina fell in love with them, she falls out of love the moment she understands they are traitors," explained Ogunjiofor. "And then like the absolute ruler she was, those men were executed."

Since Amina remained unmarried until she died, her reputation was further tarnished. "They turned around and said she wasn't a woman in the first place, she was a hermaphrodite, she was a lesbian," said Ogunjiofor. "Those legends stuck because there was nobody who could do the side to counter it." Or at least, said Ogunjiofor, "until I showed up, twenty years ago, and began to dig back into the life and times of this precious woman."

Amina, he told me, was the progenitor of the principles of democracy under which the people of Zaria live today. She opened up the trade routes. She provided for widows and orphans. She was a military strategist. She knew how to use "bows and arrows, javelins, spears, cutlasses, and machetes." According to Ogunjiofor, Amina "devised the idea of using poisonous herbs with snake venoms" and rubbing them on the tips of her weapons so her enemies would die slow, agonizing deaths after the merest scratch. "So the legend spread: Once you go to war anybody who will encounter her will die." She ruled for thirty-four years.

Ogunjiofor started researching his movie on Queen Amina twenty years ago, after the World Conference on Women in Beijing in 1995. "Amina represents all the women in the world who are downtrodden and whose rights have been maligned," he said. After the kidnappings in Chibok he saw a parallel, that "the same fate that the custodians of tradition of five hundred years ago meted out to Amina are what the Chibok girls are suffering now in the name of education." He saw Amina's story not as a northern Nigerian story but as a global one. He decided to shoot

the movie with high sound and picture quality, and to do so in
Jos, the gateway city to Northern Nigeria, with a cast of stars
from Kannywood, as Nollywood's Hausa-language industry,
based in Kano, is called.

Ojukwu, the director, had grown up here in Jos, which main-
tained a movie theater into the mid-1980s. Ojukwu would
hang out there, cleaning the hall in exchange for admission and
watching the Chinese and Indian films that were the cinema's
repertoire. He learned how to load a projector and eventually
built a projector himself with some friends. They would screen
Bollywood prints without sound in his father's garage for the
neighborhood kids.

He released his first movie in 1993, a religious story called
*Ichabod: the Glory Has Departed from Israel* commissioned by
the Catholic Biblical Movement. By the time Ogunjiofor called
Ojukwu to see if he was interested in making *Queen Amina* he
had made sixteen movies. His most recent, *'76*, a drama set amid
the turmoil that followed the assassination of General Murtala
Mohammed, was a labor of love, shot on 16mm film, which meant
that it took him five years to make. Ojukwu had planned to take a
break after wrapping *'76*, but he received a text from Ogunjiofor
about *Amina*, took three days off, then began the work.

He told me he joined to work with Ogunjiofor: "Being a
pioneer in the movie industry I just said to myself, whatever
this man wants I'm going to be involved with it because it's
somebody I respect so much."

Many of the crew belonged to what might be called the
freshman class of Nollywood. I met Millicent Jack, whom

54    Ogunjiofor described as "the first costume designer in the country." A former student of theater arts, she found her way into the industry in 1993. She had since done costumes for over a hundred Nollywood movies. On a tablet computer she showed me archival images she had used in researching the fifteenth-century Hausa costumes in *Queen Amina*—the *babariga* worn by the emirs, the *ya-chiki* (shirt) and the *wondo* (trousers), the *alkeba*, a cloak worn over the top. Crossed ropes held the tunics of the warriors in place. Her hotel room was also the wardrobe, and she slept surrounded by costumes on hangers, piles of jewelry, rows of shoes, fake fur pelts, and garments of suede. "It gladdens my heart to dress people," she said.

In the adjacent room was the workshop of Sele O. Sele, the propmaster, a tall man with long dreadlocks. He had also found his way to the industry in the mid-1990s and had worked on major Nollywood productions like *Invasion 1897* about the invasion of the kingdom of Benin, and a movie called *Up Creek Without a Paddle* about the struggle over oil in the Niger Delta. His room was filled with shields meant to look like they had been made from animal skins, and with bows and arrows. He showed me a set of manacles and chains he had sent to be made, to be worn by Amina's captured prisoners. Amina, he said, "was obsessed with gold." On this production he had three assistants. He had a bandage on his toe and I noticed an envelope of X-rays stuck between his bedframe and the wall. Later, as he trimmed the wicks of some homemade torches for an evening shoot, we chatted outside. It turned out he had been driving at night with the car full of props and been waylaid by robbers. He

had floored the accelerator, he said, and the bandits had shot   55
him in the foot.

The head of the hair and makeup department introduced himself by a single name, Gabazzini. He told he me had done makeup for "well over three hundred to five hundred movies."

I couldn't meet the set designer, who had had to leave production to attend his father's funeral, but Ogunjiofor took me to see the mud palace they had built as a set a few blocks from the Hill Station Hotel. We went on foot, trekking the three blocks to the set.

"This is where Amina and her father reigned supreme over thirteen emirates," said Ogunjiofor, when we arrived at the impressive terra cotta palace. "It's not home video," he said of the movie. "We want to be sure that this is different."

The palace was built of mud on the site of a ruin and took six months to construct. During the rainy season it had collapsed twice, but now it had stopped raining for the winter, and the walls were holding firm. He showed me the gladiatorial arena, the stocks where slaves were held, the throne from which Queen Amina ruled. The movie, he said proudly, had a cast and crew of 450 people. "It's not been done before." He told me of fight scenes with more than 200 people, some on horseback. They had hired choreographers and swordfighters, who trained the actors for two months in the hotel. They had trailers of horses and handlers. They had drones to record epic battle scenes from above "with anything any film crew can have."

"It's a hit movie," said Ogunjiofor. "We don't intend to spare costs, we don't intend to spare quality." The color grading will

56    be done in England. "We need to prove a point," he said. "We will
      stand toe to toe with any movie that's been done in Africa."

On December 1, the weather changed. The temperature dropped
to the low seventies. A dry wind began to blow, and the air was
filled with a dust that reddened the eyes and parched the throat.
This was the *harmattan*, the seasonal trade wind that blows
from the Sahara over West Africa in the winter months, dis-
rupting air travel and halving the time it took to dry a freshly
laundered t-shirt on a clothesline.

The drop in temperature coincided with an all-night shoot
for the cast and crew of *Queen Amina*. They gathered in the
parking lot of the Hill Station Hotel in late afternoon to await
transportation to the set, prepared for a plunge in temperature into the low sixties, maybe even fifties, in an extraordinary
array of rarely used cold-weather clothing: a varsity jacket, a
hunting fleece patterned with deer, an Inspector Gadget—style
khaki trench coat.

We arrived at the cow pasture around 5:00 p.m. Bonfires
were lit against the cold night. They prepared for a scene in
which a group of assassins dressed like ninjas steal into a hut
and murder Amina's lover, then a scene where Amina discovers
the killing. "You first let out a scream," Ojukwu told the actor,
Lucy Ameh. "Then a wail."

There was no craft services, no bowls of candy or piles
of bananas, no trailers in which to warm themselves, just the
assortment of Toyota Camrys and other cars in which we
arrived. As a VIP visitor I was given an upturned apple crate

and a spot by the fire, for which I was grateful. There were no toilets, and people brought flashlights into the bushes to relieve themselves, heeding warnings to look out for reptiles. The mood was jovial.

A crowd of women and children from a nearby neighborhood gathered under a tree to watch, bundled in blankets. As the crew set up the first shot, a partylike atmosphere emerged, with production members roasting corn around their campfire, and singing songs. A line producer played Candy Crush on her phone. The warrior princess with the Mohawk stood to one side and practiced her lines. The shoot was delayed by problems with the sound—the truck with the generator had to park too close to the set because the production didn't have the cables to run the lights—and with the lighting—bulbs kept shattering because of power surges from a frayed cord. It was 10:00 p.m. before they shot a scene of *Amina* in hand-to-hand sword combat with a band of invaders dressed like the ninjas in *Mortal Kombat*—red turbans that revealed only their eyes and blue pajamas.

The hours passed. "Every spirit of slumber, out of this place!" said the assistant director, when he clapped the clapper. The ninjas missed their cue to steal into the hut. I was cold, and found my way to the backseat of a parked sedan, where I lay down to sleep. I awoke around 3:00 a.m. to clamor and shouting outside the car. A lantern had fallen over in a hut crafted from sticks and set it on fire. The crew decided to wrap for the night.

Nollywood moviemakers were used to setbacks, so the shoot would continue. As Ojukwu said, "We do not have a level

58    playing ground but that's not an excuse." A few weeks later, *Queen Amina* was in the can, and expected to be released by late 2017.

I returned to Lagos the following afternoon. The *harmattan* had reached here, too. The humidity had broken and a brown haze hung in the sky.

## 30 DAYS IN ATLANTA (2014)
### DIRECTED BY ROBERT O. PETERS

*30 Days in Atlanta* is a comedy about the clash of cultures that happens when a pair of Nigerian cousins travels to America. Richard, played by Ramsey Nouah, is an urbane IT consultant in Lagos who receives a visit from his provincial cousin, Akpos, played by the comedian Ayo "AY" Makun. Akpos is from Warri, the Delta State city that one Nigerian described to me as the favorite setting of "comedy and ghettolike movies," explaining that "a person from Warri will always make jokes about everything around him."

The cousins win their trip to Atlanta as the grand prize in a raffle. New clothes are bought for the journey; Richard's ex tries to regain his attention; and Akpos's mom comes to bid farewell, bringing a bounty of dried fish, potash, palm fruit, and a live goat so the cousins don't starve to death in the United States.

"Who has time to apply for a visa for a goat?" cries Richard.

The first clue that taking a Nigerian out of his country can cause a shift in the known order happens at Hartsfield-Jackson International Airport, when the duo are shocked to see a celebrated Nigerian prosperity preacher, the sort who promises church donations will lead to personal wealth, dragging his own luggage. "That bag could be loaded with dollars," suggests Richard. "One can never be sure with our ministers."

America is a land of suburban McMansions, disobedient children, and women who pay for their dinners on dates ("It's

60 called *going dotch*," explains Richard to a scandalized Akpos). Couples make out in public and men have to cook for their bossy wives and change diapers for their babies. When the pair get carded at a bar, Akpos is appalled. "Call Obama!" he tells the bartender. "Obama na drink beer?" They are surprised to find that a friend who claimed to work in the oil business in fact pumps gas. Akpos even gets arrested after pulling a broken bottle while playing a dice game. "A weapon?" he protests. "We use broken bottles to exchange pleasantries!"

It wouldn't be a comedy without some romantic interests, and soon the men are nicely paired up. But when Akpos's girl-friend hears him bragging to his friends back home about get-ting a green card, she kicks him out of the house. "It's normal boastful talk in Warri!" he says helplessly. All's well that ends well: The cousins' new American girlfriends decide to return with them to Nigeria to meet their families.

At the time of its release, *30 Days in Atlanta* was the highest-grossing Nigerian cinema release in the country's history. It helped that the cast was packed with big Nollywood names, and the movie even landed American actor Vivica A. Fox, who plays the domineering American wife of a Nigerian uncle. The Nige-rian abroad is a popular theme for a country with such a large diaspora, and it's the subject of both comedies like *Osuofia in London* (2003) and *Baby Oku in America* (2013) and deportation dramas like *Anchor Baby* (2010). According to the U.S. Census Bureau, more than 375,000 Nigerians lived in the United States in 2015, and the cultural misunderstandings depicted in *30 Days* resonate widely, as almost every Nigerian would have lived or have family who lived abroad. The comedy in the movie simultaneously exaggerates and defuses stereotypes about emigrants, and jokes at the expense of the host culture remind Nigerians of their own values. Akpos's mishaps even offer a kind of translation of Nollywood and Nigeria to non-Nigerian audiences.

In 2016, AY's second travel movie, *A Trip to Jamaica*, broke *30 Days in Atlanta*'s own box office records. The most recent installment, *10 Days in Sun City*, where AY goes to Johannesburg, came out in 2017. These destinations are not arbitrary—the southern United States, the Caribbean, and South Africa are epicenters of Nollywood's non-Nigerian fan base, and the AY franchise addresses these communities directly.

# Pirates and Traders

The Alaba International Market for Electronics is located off the Badagry Expressway, the transport corridor that goes west out of Lagos to the border with Benin. When I traveled on the Badagry to Alaba for the first time, in mid-November 2015, there was nothing express about the expressway. The road was choked with Volkswagen Transporters, Ford Transits, and HiAce Super vans, all painted school bus yellow, with inspirational mottoes on their windshields such as NO KING AS GOD or APPRICIATION. The vehicles arrayed across its haphazard lanes inched forward at a pace just slightly slower than a woman sauntering in a pink and purple abaya down the highway median.

Around the cars, people sold things. In an hour locked in a bottleneck under a bridge I saw hawkers selling plastic folders, Q-tips, a map of Nigeria decorated with all of its past presidents, dishtowels, umbrellas, phone chargers for the car, cologne, peanuts in their shells, plantain chips, compact discs,

chewing gum, newsboy caps, and mini fire extinguishers. They    63
sold books that reflected Nigeria's obsessions with Christianity, positive thinking, and material success (*Me and My Big
Mouth!* by Joyce Meyer, *Attitude is Everything, How to Write Business Proposals*—but also *Things Fall Apart* by Chinua Achebe).
I saw an exercise apparatus called a Tummy Trimmer. I saw a
dartboard, a chess set, Scrabble, boxes of tissues, and leather
sandals. I bought a baggie of roasted cashews from a woman carrying a plastic tub of them on her head.

The air on the road was hazy from diesel fumes. The sky
was gray with cloud formations that threatened a rain that never
came. Alongside this highway another, newer highway was
being built. Nigerian workers painted black and white stripes on
its barriers, overseen by Chinese supervisors. The new highway
was a kind of promise: that Lagos could change, that one day
this horrible traffic jam would be replaced by a speedy light rail
system, that there was some kind of momentum toward greater
ease and comfort, toward an electricity grid that worked, toward
highways that were not rutted, and toward movies with excellent sound quality.

The road passed Bible Wonderland, Ltd., a concrete gate
that read WELCOME TO FESTAC TOWN, a patch of brilliantly green
tropical foliage, carpenters selling furniture, and marketers
selling live chickens and their eggs, pyramids of tomatoes and of
hot peppers. Graffiti on road barriers advertised web design services and cures for erectile dysfunction. STOP MESSING THIS PLACE
UP U WILL BE CAUGHT, read the spray paint over a pile of garbage in
a ditch. We passed the Dominion Faith International Ministry,

64    falling-down houses, and a promotion for a "War Against
Satanic Manipulation Preaching Session."

Exiting the highway for the market was accomplished not
via cloverleaf or overpass but by a sheared-off U-turn into
the oncoming rush of yellow transport vans with fare takers
hanging off the sides. We drove past an area of two- and three-
story buildings with facades of faded paint, snarled electrical
wires, the trundling mechanical tricycles known as *keke napeps*
(also schoolbus yellow), mobile phone stores, and purveyors of
electronics and umbrellas. A motorbike taxi pulled up alongside
the car, a photograph of a smiling blond baby mysteriously glued
to its engine.

The driver who brought me to Alaba, Solomon Iseowula,
parked the car in a guarded yard and shouted down a man
who was aggressively promoting himself to be our fixer in the
market. (The man would, explained Solomon, want to take a
cut of anything we bought, thereby inflating the prices.) Alaba
is a vast maze of passageways. It is the major wholesale electronics market serving the region, the place where the contents
of thousands of cargo containers from Asia offload their cables,
cords, Bluetooth headsets, and mobile phones for distribution around Africa's most populous country. We walked from
the market's edge down a passageway that was lined with stalls
selling Nollywood videos of all kinds. Banners hung from above
advertising a movie called *Wanted*, and another called *Emily
Millionaire*. I had come with a list of movies I wanted to buy, but
Solomon avoided many of the stalls as we went past, steering
me toward a man he would later tell me he selected because he

looked to be of morally upstanding character. ("He's clean, he's well-shaven," Solomon explained.)

The marketer's name was Barnabas Mbanugo. He was a middle-aged man with an avuncular air, wearing dark jeans and a white button-down shirt. After the gracious and formal greeting that one receives on entering any shop or home in Nigeria—"you are welcome"—I handed him my list. He peered at it through reading glasses then began pulling titles off the shelves and from boxes in the back. Vendors like Mbanugo were the movie industry's connection with the informal market. Every month, the Association of Movie Producers or independent distribution companies would negotiate with the marketers over release dates, determining which marketers would be allowed to distribute which movies. As a man down the passageway started enthusiastically praising Jesus into a loudspeaker for the noonday prayer, Mbanugo showed me a monthly manifest from one such agreement, which described which films would be distributed by which marketers, and the location of their market stalls.

Alaba was primarily a wholesale market: Once Mbanugo got copies of a movie, he would, from his stall, disperse them to other sellers across Lagos. If he bought the movies from the producers for 200 naira apiece he would then sell them to his marketers for 250 naira each. The sellers would in turn sell to their customers for 300 naira. I bought fourteen DVDs from Mbanugo, which ranged in price from 250 naira for a Yoruba-language horror movie called *B'ogiri O Lanu* (translated from Yoruba as *Without a Crack in the Wall*) to 350 and even 400 naira for higher-end

66　"New Nollywood" movies that had been released in the cinemas, like *30 Days in Atlanta* and Kunle Afolayan's *Phone Swap*.

I had not bought a DVD in the United States for years and my computer no longer had a drive to play them, but in Nigeria, DVDs and video CDs were not obsolete technologies. Cellular data and cable television were expensive here. Broadband availability was minimal. The fraction of the population who owned computers and could afford Internet access tended to rely on little pay-as-you-go satellite dongles, which groups of friends sometimes pooled together to buy. The Internet access via these small black boxes was excellent, but streaming movies on them was a way to eat through expensive data at an alarming rate, and one often stared at a buffering symbol more than an actual movie. Still, many people watched movies on their cell phones. Downloaded from the Internet by a single person who paid for a fast connection or accessed one at work, these movies could be passed on to friends and family via peer-to-peer Bluetooth file-sharing apps without eating into data allowances. But watching a movie on a cell phone is not the best experience of most movies, even if it is certainly a better experience of sitting on public transportation in an endless traffic jam. There was also cable: On television, the big satellite cable networks had channels dedicated to Nollywood, but these too had limited reach as the subscriptions were expensive for most Nigerians. As of 2015, the most popular African pay TV network, South Africa–based MultiChoice, had only an estimated 1.2 million subscribers in Nigeria.

So, for content that wasn't on cable, and when they did not want to watch movies on their cell phones, Nigerians rich and poor still consumed movies on DVDs and video CDs, many of them from Hollywood or Bollywood. Pirated foreign films and television shows were easy to find. I was hosted in Lagos by a Nigerian American friend who while I stayed with him was binge watching HBO's *Game of Thrones*, or rather, as the DVD sleeve put it, *Game of Throne*, starring, if one judged by the photos on the sleeve, Elijah Wood as Frodo Baggins. When I bought a pirated copy of Danny Boyle's *Steve Jobs* from a hawker on the bridge connecting Ikoyi to Victoria Island, I did so in the blind hope that I would get that movie instead of, as the front of the DVD sleeve indicated, its soundtrack or, as the back of the sleeve advertised, Alex Gibney's documentary about Steve Jobs. When you bought a pirated movie or television show in Nigeria, you weren't making a decision to buy something illegally because it was cheaper, you simply wanted to watch something. In the absence of cheap Internet streaming or a plethora of cineplexes, it was often the case that the *only* way to access a particular piece of content was to find it on the street on DVD or video CD. When it came to Hollywood, local taste heavily favored shows and movies with African American leads, and the shows I saw the hawkers selling the most during my time in Nigeria were *Empire* and *Scandal*.

Solomon Iseowula, the driver who transported me around Lagos for the duration of my visit, had an iPhone and at least one other mobile device, but he also had a portable DVD player

68    in his Toyota Camry and a stockpile of Nollywood comedies
and Hollywood action thrillers to watch while waiting for clients. When he took me shopping for movies in the markets, he
would often buy some DVDs for himself. A friend told me that
her hairstylist, who made house calls in Lagos, would bring Nollywood movies on disc to watch as she braided hair. Nigerians
could buy DVDs and video CDs in neighborhood stalls or from
street hawkers who wandered between cars stuck in traffic, and
I bought many movies from these vendors with varying results
in quality. (The biggest downside of watching on a DVD, in my
experience, was trying to find your place again after the power
cut out in the middle of the movie, which in Lagos would usually happen multiple times during the course of a viewing. Nollywood DVDs did not divide the movies into chapters, which
meant that every power cut meant several minutes of fast forwarding when the lights came back on.)

Nollywood began in the market—here, in Alaba. It created its vast audience by an effective market-based distribution system first of VHS tapes and later of digital discs. Even in
2015, the satellite cable audience, the cinema audience, and the
Internet audience had yet to reach the size of the disc-buying
audience.

But many Nollywood producers and directors, especially
those of bigger budget movies, had come, by necessity, to ignore
this audience. They would talk to me about the potential of cinemas, satellite cable networks, and digital subscription platforms like iRoko and Netflix, even though such platforms would
only be accessible to a fraction of their viewers in Nigeria and

around Africa (outside of Africa was another matter.) These producers ignored the disc-buying audience because piracy meant that they made very little money from them.

Once a movie was released into the market into a replicable format, revenue from its sales was all but lost to the people who made the movie. The fact was that in a country of 180 million people, where the audience for a popular movie on a disc or a mobile device could be in the millions, a producer might earn revenue from at most, if he or she were lucky, 200,000 or 300,000 disc sales. This was due to the rapidity with which movies would be copied from official distribution channels and enter the pirated market, where sellers, having no need to make a return on an investment, would drop prices from 300 naira to 150 naira, or even 50 naira. Having not had to put up the money for making a movie, these small sums represented almost pure profit to the pirates.

It was due in part to piracy that Nollywood's popularity had extended beyond the country's own borders. Before Nollywood movies were available to be digitally streamed, pirates distributed them around the world on disc. In 2008, as a Fulbright Scholar in Mozambique, a country on the other side of the African continent, where the *lingua franca* is Portuguese, not English, I saw Nigerian movies for sale in the north near the country's borders with Tanzania, Malawi, and Zimbabwe. The movies were also for sale in New York City, in Brooklyn and the Bronx, where they found an audience among Caribbean immigrants as well as African ones. A 2009 *New York Times* article described a store in the Bronx called the African Movies Mall, which did wholesale distribution of Nollywood movies to smaller stores catering to African and Caribbean immigrants. Even before digital piracy became a problem, most of this foreign sales revenue was lost to Nigerian producers. In 2010, for example, the Brooklyn District Attorney's office seized more than 10,000 counterfeit Nollywood movies from stores in Flatbush, Brooklyn.

Nollywood did not have a distribution problem. Its movies were widely available around the country and the world. It did not have a success problem. Nollywood was very popular. But the money made did not necessarily go to the producers who invested in the movies, because Nollywood had a piracy problem. The ad hoc distribution system that created the industry was now the biggest obstacle to its success.

"The day is gone when we used to be able to make money off of DVDs and CDs," Genevieve Nnaji told the Toronto International Film Festival in 2016. "But there's one thing we still have: eyeballs." Nnaji hoped to make up for lost revenue with cinemas. "If we had enough cinemas, like Hollywood does, we will be good because we have the numbers," she said. "Africa has—forget Nigeria—Africa has enough people to be able to buy tickets."

I asked Barnabas Mbanugo if he had a copy of Kunle Afolayan's movie *October 1*. Set in the waning days of colonial rule, it is a detective story about the hunt for a serial killer who goes on a murderous spree as the British prepare hand over control of the country to Nigerians, and was a highly anticipated "New Nollywood" movie released in the cinema in 2014. He told me it was not yet available on DVD. I had seen the movie for sale several times on the highway, and I soon learned that *October 1* had been pirated even before its official cinema release, probably by someone in the post-production facility.

Afolayan had other possibilities for revenue for his high-end movie. It had been released in cinemas and he had secured an international distribution deal with Netflix. But the vast majority of Nollywood movies did not have much possibility for earning revenue outside of disc sales, beyond the relatively low license fees paid by cable channels. In the market for lower-budget B-movies that had to earn all of their revenue from disc sales, the producers clearly held some control over the market, or they would have had to stop making movies altogether. I heard of different strategies to maintain control. Taiwo Samuel, who produced a Yoruba-language horror movie I bought in Alaba, told me that his strategy was to print an official DVD jacket that marketers had to pay him to receive. A New Nollywood producer named Mildred Okwo said she makes the marketers pay her a fee based on projected sales before she hands over a master. Ishaya Bako, the director of *Road to Yesterday*, told me the production had contemplated "pirating themselves"—flooding the market with their own low-cost copies. One popular director, Lancelot Oduwa Imasuen, circulated a public warning for his movie *ATM*.

PIRACY ALARM! PIRACY ALARM!! PIRACY ALARM!!! it read. "Well-meaning Nigerians are advised to disregard and do not purchase the pirated copies being circulated by some unscrupulous elements on major streets and on the road during traffic."

*

The financial disconnect between producers and their audiences also meant that the primary way to know which Nollywood movies were the most popular—not with the limited cinema or satellite cable audiences, but with the disc-watching nation and Africa at large—was by word of mouth. Consider an Igbo-language comedy called *Nkoli Nwa Nsukka*. When I asked Shaibu Husseini, an academic and movie critic for *The Guardian* newspaper of Nigeria, what he thought was the most popular movie in recent years, he said he thought *Nkoli* might be one because he had attended the burial of the producer's father and it had been extremely lavish.

When I bought the movie at Idumota Market in downtown Lagos I learned a second metric of Nollywood success: *Nkoli Nwa Nsukka*, the first installment of which had first come out in 2014, now had at least fifteen sequels. I read articles about the new SUV that its star, Rachael Okonkwo, had bought, and about her appearance at a charity event sponsored by Rapha juice, for which she served as brand ambassador. But there was no central database, no Excel spreadsheet in a computer with the exact numbers. There were no critical reviews of the movie in any major newspapers that I could find. The metrics by which I, an American, would try to gauge a movie's popularity or success did not apply to Nigeria's fragmented market. And the number of sequels attested to the rapidity with which the revenue of the movie's iterations, once released and pirated, was out of the hands of the producers who made it.

The producers and directors of Nollywood railed about piracy. Some had organized street protests to demand the government crack down on it. Others were so bored with the subject that they dismissed earning money from their disc-buying audience as a lost cause. Then there were those who had to deal with it directly, because they were in the business of distributing DVDs. They, at least, had not yet given up on the business.

One day in December, as the *harmattan* choked Lagos in a smog that hid the stilt city on the lagoon from the Third Mainland Bridge, I returned to Badagry, in the neighborhood of Alaba Market, to visit Gabriel Okoye. Better known by his Slavic-sounding nickname, Gabosky, Okoye had been a Nollywood distributor and executive producer since the mid-1990s. More recently, he won a loan from the Nigerian Bank of Industry to develop a system of licensed disc distributors that would allow producers to bypass pirates via more formal and controllable channels. In an interview he gave to the magazine *Yes! International*, Gabosky described his attempts to control the pirates:

*I started arresting them; I went to Alaba to arrest them. They started fighting openly and telling me I cannot control piracy. We fought and later what I did was to withdraw. A year later, I did not release my film, after October 1. I did not release any film until December 15, 2015. I released* Headgone, *October 1, and* The Needle. *They were also pirated. I could not do anything, then 15 February, 2016, a day after Valentine['s Day], I released* Invasion 1937, *by Lancelot Oduwa Imasuen. A week after, they also pirated it. I said no, I traced it. So, I said let me give them a small fight again. I traced it to a guy, I got him arrested on the road, because if you go inside Alaba market, they will machete you. They have all kinds of weapons and they don't care who you are. The last time I went there, they macheted one of the policemen that came with me to raid the market and the policeman was so traumatized. So, I decided to lay ambush outside the market and luckily he was going to cargo goods for someone in Benin. That was how we got him arrested at Ohonba Line's park and handed him over to the Ojo police station. That same day, they wanted to grant him bail. I asked them why, they said their boss gave an order that no culprit should be in cell for more than 24 hours. So, we contacted the Copyright Commission and we handed him over to Copyright Commission and later we contacted industry people.*

Gabosky's reputation was shrouded in mythology. Nollywood producers would repeat rumors that he had once been a pirate in Alaba himself, in the bad old days of copied foreign movies on VHS. For those movie producers who preferred to remain removed from the fray, Gabosky was a liaison to Nigeria's urban marketplaces. He knew who was playing by the rules in the market and who was pirating his movies. Barnabas Mbanugo, at least, followed Gabosky's rules when he told me that *October 1*, pirated copies of which I had seen being sold by many street vendors in Lagos, had not yet been released on DVD. Gabosky's company G-Media was its official distributor.

Gabosky's office was in an area of warehouses not far from Alaba, along a dirt road as hummocky as a motocross course, ancient cargo trucks beached along its edges like whales. We

drove past a truck with leaping dolphins painted across the
cab, then one with a mural of Jesus weeping tears of blood. We
passed God With Us Plaza and the Celestial Church of Christ.
A man reclined on his motorbike under a beach umbrella, chatting on the phone. Tufted leather couches were lined up for
sale in the open air.

The headquarters of G-Media was a new-looking building
made out of green and orange panels that said GABOSKY in gold
letters across the front. A weight room was visible through the
tinted windows of the ground floor. I asked at the front gate,
having made an appointment, but was told Gabosky had not yet
arrived. My driver, a man of few words named Bisi who worked
for Solomon when the latter had too many clients, parked the
car under a tree out front. While we waited, he hailed a man
walking down the road in mechanic's overalls and hired him to
fix the car horn, which was insufficiently loud, and another man
carrying a leather kit to give him a pedicure. I was sitting in the
backseat reading the newspapers, he was having his toenails cut
in front, and the mechanic was tinkering with the horn when a
chrome-gilled banana-yellow Hummer pulled up behind us. We
turned and stared. "He is here," announced Bisi.

This was Gabosky, who tapped gently on my window. He
greeted me with a half-hug, half back pat. He wore a snakeskin
baseball cap over a du-rag, a black t-shirt, black jeans printed
with a white pattern, and black Air Jordan Nikes. I followed him
into GABOSKY, INC., past a dimly lit warehouse room filled to its
rafters with boxes of DVDs. At the front desk, three employees
lined up to greet him. As they exchanged good mornings, he

76    gave each one the same half-hug salutary gesture, almost mili-
taristic in its formality. He continued up the stairs, not pausing
to look back when I was detained to sign in to a visitor's book. A
sack of oat flour was mysteriously displayed on the front desk.

His office was painted in the same green and orange color
scheme, and filled with DVDs, honorary plaques, and gilt awards.
Here, too, boxes of instant oatmeal were carefully displayed, and a
shrink-wrapped pallet of oats was sitting on a coffee table.

Gabosky came to Lagos from eastern Nigeria. He studied
political science at the University of Nigeria in Nsukka, then
began his business career as an electronics trader in Alaba in
the early 1990s. He had a supply of VHS cassette tapes from
Asia that he would dub with foreign films and sell as packaged
movies. But it was hard to get the foreign films. "We had to
look inward and say, *Why can't we make our own content and put
it inside the cassettes?"* he explained.

After the success of *Living in Bondage*, Gabosky became the
executive producer of Ogunjiofor's popular hit *Nneka the Pretty
Serpent*. He went on to produce his own movies, including *Battle
of Musanga*, which he claims was the first in a now-established
genre of Nollywood historical epics. Today he is known primarily as a distributor or, as he put it, "the only structured and
biggest content acquisitor and DVD/VCD distributor across
Africa and the diaspora."

Gabosky's distribution network spans almost every Nigerian state; the West African countries of Ghana, Sierra Leone,
Gambia, and Cameroon; east into Congo, Rwanda, Tanzania,

Kenya; and beyond, into "most African countries." These days G-Media distributes mostly high-end movies: those that most closely resemble a Hollywood format. His catalogue includes many of the minority of Nollywood movies that had cinema releases. Because these are among the few Nollywood movies that could be called "destination movies" (most Nollywood consumers don't really seek out a particular title) they are also the first target of all the pirates.

"They prepare themselves and wait for me," he said. "They go on the Internet. They download photos. They print their jackets. And they wait." He grabbed a pile of seized copies of pirated versions of his movies, including *October 1*, and began flipping through it. "Once they hear that I've acquired the movie they know that movie's good." A successful Nollywood movie will sell 200,000 to 500,000 copies. If you factor in piracy, a movie could sell more than two million copies in Nigeria alone. It is for this reason that some Nollywood producers no longer especially care about the market that created the industry. Instead, they search for more reliable revenue streams.

Gabosky knew that in the rest of the world the DVD is a more or less obsolete technology, but what was going on in the rest of the world has not yet impacted Nigeria. As long as data is expensive, "the whole world might be doing digital and the DVD will be the thing in Africa," he said. The vast majority of Africans who connect to the Internet do so on their phones, and there are millions more phones on the continent than there are televisions. But Gabosky was not worried about

78    entrepreneurs who are betting that one day the mobile phone will be the primary outlet by which African consumers watch Nollywood movies.

"I cannot see an African man adopting to watch movie on phone," he said. "They aggregate themselves in a video viewing center, what you call community cinema. They prefer it to looking at the movie like this, because Africa likes interaction, they like being together in a communal way. This laptop audience is individualistic and Africa does not enjoy that kind of life."

He concluded: "I cannot say that DVD will be an old thing in Africa."

I asked him about the bags of oatmeal.

"Oats are one of the wonder foods," he said, and then my visit was over.

The traffic in Lagos is famously bad. The local driving culture dictates tailgating, honking, flashing of brights, left turns into oncoming traffic, passing on the right, and shouting (but no cursing or lewd gestures—not in such a religious country). It isn't rare to see a car casually reversing down an on-ramp, a motorcycle scattering pedestrians on a sidewalk, or a truck inching over a highway median to make an improbable u-turn. Drivers honk to simply acknowledge each other, like flocks of migratory geese; they flash their brights like they are issuing ship signals in Morse code. Turn signals are far less enthusiastically deployed. Pedestrians in Nigeria have no right of way. In Lagos driving culture there is no such thing as right of way, a problem when constant power outages mean traffic lights are frequently out.

The best way to avoid a traffic jam in Lagos is to avoid traveling from the mainland to the islands in the morning and going the other direction in the evening, when the lines of idling commuter vehicles span the length of the Third Mainland Bridge. But there are certain days when the entire city is all but shut down. The jams on the day of my visit to Gabosky were epic in scope, and it took hours to get back to where I was staying in Ikoyi from Badagry. A fuel shortage—a difficult phenomenon to explain in one of the world's largest oil-exporting countries—had been affecting the country since I had arrived three weeks before. Most mornings outside my window, a line of cars stretched from the gas station on the corner all the way down the street. Drivers who were simply trying to continue down the street would bypass the gas line by pulling into the lane for oncoming traffic. This would result in standoffs with cars traveling the other direction, and shouting matches in which bystanders and pedestrians would enthusiastically involve themselves until one group of vehicles would finally concede to reverse from whence they came to let traffic through. (One driver who made a principled stand not to reverse was roundly shouted at by strangers walking down the street. "He thinks he is a big Nigerian man," muttered one pedestrian, with scorn.) Once they started backing up, long lines of cars moving in reverse would meet other cars coming down the street, with the mechanical tricycles trying to shortcut via the sidewalk, and the honking would start up again. It was a daily spectacle that eased only when the station's gas ran out or on Sundays, when the clamorous city would fall silent and churchgoing pedestrians strolled peacefully in their finery.

On this day, the fuel shortage had extended to the express-ways. The entry to the petrol depots in Apapa was backed up with empty fuel trucks that had been parked for hours, even days. Lagos Traffic Radio, a call-in station where people described the traffic jams they had hit in animated pidgin English, was flooded with reports. The main arteries were all but stopped. We idled behind a tricycle with a particularly existential slogan on the back: CAN YOU PASS GOD.

Lagos traffic was frequently referenced in Nollywood movies, along with reckless motorcycle taxi drivers, *keke* tricycle drivers who try to overcharge, and self-styled preachers who deliver zealous sermons to trapped passengers in crowded vans. A few days later, I saw an article about a Nollywood movie written by a reporter who had not managed to watch the movie before writing her feature. "The actual order of event was for the reporter to be at the screenings," she wrote. "But with the help of non-moving trucks and their drivers along Creek Road, Apapa, it became 'mission impossible.'"

## TAXI DRIVER: OKO ASHEWO (2015)
## DIRECTED BY DANIEL ORIAHI

*Taxi Driver* is a movie about a taxi driver and a prostitute. It's a comedy, a dark one.

The driver is Adigun (Femi Jacobs), a naïve newcomer to Lagos who has left his hometown of Ibadan to inherit his dead father's taxi. Adigun works nights, and soon has a steady customer, Delia (Ijeoma Grace Agu), a sex worker who has to crisscross the city each night to see her clients. In another nod to Martin Scorsese's 1976 classic, Delia wears a Mohawk, like Travis Bickle's, but one dyed pink and purple. She is scornful of Adigun's provincialism, and calls him a "Johnny-just-come." Adigun, in turn, disapproves of her line of work, despite depending on her for gas money.

*Taxi Driver*, like many New Nollywood movies made for a cosmopolitan urban audience, abandons the moral simplicity typical of older Nollywood movies. Delia reaches the end of the movie without finding Jesus and renouncing her profession; Adigun does not win or lose a fortune, hit his head and get amnesia, succumb to a curse, or fall into a cult. Instead, *Taxi Driver* integrates certain tropes of Nollywood into a more globalized cinematic vision, where a story is not meant to teach a lesson but rather to produce a mood, to capture the subtle visual reality of a particular place. In addition to Scorsese, Oriahi was inspired by Jim Jarmusch's *Night on Earth*, and the sensibility here could be described as art house. Delia was styled to

82  look like Grace Jones. The movie takes place almost entirely at
night, where Lagos is shadowy, its streetlights tinged blue. But
the movie does not abandon its roots—there is, for example, a
ghost—a Shakespearean omen and a throwback to the encounters with the otherworldly so common in classic Nollywood
movies.

"I dreamt I saw my father," Adigun recounts to the friend
who is teaching him to navigate Lagos. "He was smiling, then
suddenly he started bleeding everywhere."

His friend looks at him.

"Enjoy Lagos," he says. "When you get to that junction,
drop me."

The actors switch between Yoruba and Nigerian pidgin, the
language of the streets. Usually only the Yoruba lines would
carry English subtitles, but here the pidgin comes subtitled
too, in standard written English, presumably for the benefit of
non-Nigerians.

The end of *Taxi Driver* is a little muddled: Some money is
stolen, Delia is kidnapped, there is a car chase through Lagos
and a shootout, but the movie is carried by its soundtrack of
Yoruba pop music, its wry but funny script, and Femi Jacobs's
performance as the heavy-lidded, naïve driver. It evokes the
dream of Lagos as a place where people from all over Nigeria
come to seek a better life, but the Lagos of *Taxi Driver* is as
unforgiving as the New York of *Midnight Cowboy*. As a gang
boss crossed by Adigun puts it, "In Lagos you need to be smart
to survive. Nothing here happens without the knowledge of

the underworld." The sweet-natured Adigun tries to disagree, but the boss insists: "We make Lagos what it is, without us Lagos would be boring. It's bad people like us with a little good that guard the system."

# Digital Futures

Jason Njoku was born in England to Nigerian parents but was late to Nollywood, discovering it for the first time in 2009, when he was twenty-nine years old. After a failed attempt at starting a magazine in Manchester, Njoku had moved back home, to his childhood bedroom in London, to live with his mother, who spent a lot of time watching Nigerian movies on DVD. Njoku didn't care especially for the movies, but he was intrigued by the amount of time his mother spent watching them, and the lengths she went to get them. They were not easy to find, as he discovered one day when his mother asked him to find her some more. He looked in what seemed like the obvious places: Amazon and eBay, but there was nothing online. He bought them where his mom had found them, at local mom and pop stores that served West African immigrants. The shopping experience "was just an absolute nightmare," he later remembered. "It was the worst experience in the world."

Njoku picked through a pile of discs in sleeves with collages of unknown actors, their faces fixed in dramatic expressions of dismay and vengeance. The movies did not have descriptions of what they were about. Njoku had no way to gauge which movie was good and which was bad. The directors did not seem to have any particular reputation or draw. There was often no mention of who directed a movie at all, or who starred in it. A producer might be listed across the bottom, as in "a Tchidi Chikere Production," but who was that? What did that mean? Plot summaries were vague. (This is the jacket copy on a DVD called *Affection*: "A rich man had three sons whom he loved unequaled due to the evil mind of the first son. The first son never love his father but his money so he plot to kill his father with the aid of his daughter and only son.")

"There's no systematic marketing behind any particular movie," said Njoku. "It's a lean back experience where it's like 'whatever's there, I'll watch it, and it's going to be kind of okay.' That's the experience."

Njoku saw potential for a business. At the very least he could sell the movies on the Internet and offer some organizing principles that might indicate genre, plot, and quality.

First he started a store on eBay selling DVDs. The store failed. For reasons that evaded him, the people who wanted to watch Nollywood movies on DVD did not want to buy them online. Those who did buy from him were far from immigrant communities; he grew a small customer base in Wales, which indicated to him that when the mom and pop stores were not there to provide, the audience would look for the movies online, and if he could put

86     the movies on the Internet people would watch them. He decided
       on a different strategy: license Nollywood movies, broadcast
       them on YouTube, and earn money from the ad revenue.

       In 2010, Njoku bought a hundred video CDs in London,
       then followed the addresses listed on the back of them to Lagos,
       straight to Alaba, to try and figure out who owned the rights.
       There was no standardized copyright framework, no contracts,
       and no revenue arrangements. Nollywood functioned on hand-
       shake deals organized around one-time fees. Nollywood pro-
       ducers did not have entertainment lawyers. Nollywood actors
       did not have agents. "I've never seen a contract between an artist
       and a movie producer," he said. "They just don't have them."

       Njoku started licensing movies directly from producers,
       and when he bought movies he signed contracts to broadcast
       them online. To adjust to the local business culture, he closed
       his deals in unconventional ways: not just signing the contract
       but photographing the signing of the contracts, even recording
       producers stating the terms of their contracts on video. "We
       made it very difficult for people to try and fuck us," he said. At
       first the producers ignored his phone calls, but once he started
       paying, word got around the market, and soon the producers
       started calling him.

       In two weeks he bought the digital rights to two hundred
       movies from between thirty and forty producers and marketers.
       He did not discriminate. "Whatever you bring I'd buy," he said.
       "Closed my eyes and buy, wide and deep." He paid $200 for the
       rights to each movie. He asked for digital files. The producers
       laughed—there were no digital files—and handed over discs.

Once he licensed the content, he then had to rip the video from the discs and enter in the year of production and the name of the director. In addition to watching each movie to be able to write a summary, he had to cut any copyrighted music to bypass YouTube's content filter system. A movie called *Beyoncé and Rihanna*, which was about a music competition between two rivals, featured songs by the real-life Beyoncé and Rihanna, and all of them had to be cut, which meant excising the most dramatic scenes in the movie. "People still watched it," Njoku said with a shrug.

When the Nollywoodlove channel launched on YouTube in 2010, it became an almost instant success. Its database grew from thirty movies in November 2010 to a thousand just seven months later. Usage exploded to 1.6 million viewers a month, generating monthly advertising revenues of fifty thousand dollars for a small team working out of Njoku's London apartment.

It helped that at the time there was no competition, but Njoku knew the competition would come. Cable channels had to up their bids to buy content, and Nollywoodlove began an arms race with them—the price peaked at $25,000 a movie by mid-2012. Njoku realized Nollywoodlove could be producing its own content for less money.

As in every business deal in Nigeria, there were lessons to be learned. A producer might sign a contract for two movies and deliver only one, or take the money for the movie and invest it in a shipment of electronics from China instead. In other instances, a producer would promise A-list actors then deliver B-list names. Njoku might split the cost of production—he

88    would put up $25,000 and the producer would theoretically put up the same—but he soon noticed that the producer would then deliver a $25,000 movie instead of a $50,000 one. Njoku stopped giving producers any money up front, to keep them from using it to pay a family member's school fees, or to pay their rent, and to keep himself from overpaying for an inferior product. The contracts became more detailed, with stipulations about which actors had to be in it if the movie was going to be bought, and how long it would have to be.

Meanwhile, Njoku's content licenses started expiring, so the producers of the movies began putting them on YouTube themselves. They flooded the site with Nollywood content, and Nollywoodlove's business suffered.

So Njoku decided to focus on his new project, a subscription service of Nollywood movies for the African diaspora that would offer viewers exactly what Njoku could not find when he first went shopping for movies for his mom: information about the movie, some expectation of quality, and an idea about who made it.

By 2016, this business, called iRoko, had made Njoku famous. But even though iRoko was lauded in the press as "the Netflix of Africa," all the free movies available online were preventing viewers from buying paid subscriptions. Then there were the company's shortcomings in the domestic market, since the practice of laptop computers streaming movies was still marginal in Nigeria, and in Africa overall. In 2016, Netflix launched its own streaming service in Nigeria, but for most

Nigerians it was still easier to receive Nollywood movies via
disc, USB stick, Bluetooth, or cable television.

But iRoko did become an established broker between Nollywood and the outside world, selling movies to airlines and cable
channels outside of Africa and serving as a way station between
the handshake dealmaking of the Nollywood market and the
contract-based business practices of America and Europe.

And like anyone looking hard enough at the Nigerian
market, Njoku understands that the long-term future of Nollywood is the smartphone, of which analysts predict there will be
725 million on the continent by 2020.

"I think TV is really important because once you make
enough money you get a TV, right?" said Njoku. "It's an aspira-
tional thing. I don't think that changes. So as more people migrate
into the middle class that doesn't change. But there are big families in a single household, and within that single household there
might be one television. But there might be ten different mobile
devices amongst the family. So our view is that, as the media frag-
ments, people's viewing habits get much more narrow. Rather
than wanting four hundred channels or fifty channels, you might
want three or four, kind of structured around a particular content group—like telenovelas, or Nollywood in our case, or Korean
stuff. We can see that fragmentation happening, and we just hope
to be in the game participating in it."

When I visited in 2015, iRoko's offices in Ikeja employed
around a hundred people. Another two dozen or so employees
worked out of iRoko's offices in London and New York. The focus

of the company had recently shifted from courting foreign-based viewers to iRoko's subscription streaming service to courting Nigeria-based subscribers to a local app. And in this endeavor, Njoku was not alone.

In the fall of 2016, Mark Zuckerberg, the founder of Facebook, paid a two-day visit to Nigeria as part of a tour of the continent. In a speech to local entrepreneurs, he said, "One of the things I'm most excited about on my trip to Lagos is going to check out Nollywood, because I think it really is, from everything I've heard, and I hope I'm not disproven on this, but it really sounds like a national treasure." Later, in a video posted on Facebook, he gave an introduction to the industry from outside a building. "Hey everybody, we're about to go check out Nollywood, which is Nigeria's film and media industry," he said. "Let's go!"

Zuckerberg was not actually visiting Nollywood. Nollywood has no geographic center; it is not a place. Zuckerberg was in fact standing outside the offices of a startup called Afrinolly, a mobile app that its founders hope will startup profit from the millions of Africans who watch videos on their phones.

Afrinolly began in 2011 when its CEO, Chike Maduegbuna, joined an Android developer's contest sponsored by Google, and won. "We saw statistics of what Africans are searching online, both within and from the diaspora, and it turned out that African movies are up there on the list. So we kind of asked ourselves, how do you even know what movies are coming out of Nollywood? Where is our own equivalent of IMDb? And it was that concern that led us to actually develop Afrinolly for the competition." He smiled. With the $25,000 prize money, Maduegbuna and his team of developers expanded their prototype into a real app, where Nollywood fans could go to watch trailers and learn about the latest movie releases.

Like Njoku, Maduegbuna soon came to see Nollywood as an industry in need of a more formalized business model. He generated a list of possible improvements: introducing formal accounting practices, generating revenue for producers instead of pirates, streamlining the global distribution of African movies (especially around the continent), brokering better relationships between the industry and local brands, developing a more structured approach to financing movies, and more than anything, capitalizing on the potential of the vast mobile phone market of Nigeria and beyond.

When Afrinolly sponsored a short film competition, they received hundreds of submissions, and Maduegbuna became aware that younger, globalized Nigerians no longer made fun of the homespun movies their older relatives watched at home. They now saw Nigeria's own movie industry as a desirable place in which to seek success. Connecting the older generation of storytellers with a younger, more technologically aware generation of aspirants became another goal.

"It seems like we are having young emerging filmmakers who are graduates of film schools and some of them are abroad, and some of them are still trying to come back and they're all making the same African stories," he said. But the young people did not necessarily have the same talent for mass appeal. "This new generation and the old generation are not actually talking to each other. . . . The old generation doesn't understand Internet and social media but the old generation understands the cultural nuances that drive the storylines, so the old stories are a lot more economically viable than the new generation. The new generation wants to tell the story about a Lagos that looks like New York, but that's not the story that people actually want to pay to watch. People want to watch the traditional stories that have our culture embedded in it. So we found out that the old generation has the ability to create stories that can make money, but they don't understand social media and don't understand Internet. The young generation understands digital technology, they understand Internet and social media, but they were born in cities, they were not born in villages. So they were born in cities and they don't really understand the culture, so they don't speak the local language, so they can't actually drive stories that have strong cultural undertones. So at that point we thought that okay, and the industry was very chaotic. The good thing about technology is that it's easier to organize with technology. So we began to look at ourselves as we could actually contribute in this ecosystem. With technology we could actually change how things are if we could solve piracy, if we could create an economic model that would drive the commerce, and if we could help with some level of in a structured way of doing things."

I visited Maduegbuna at Afrinolly's offices in the Lagos neighborhood of Ikeja, the same ones that Zuckerberg would visit later that year. After two years of working out of Maduegbuna's house, the company had rented the facility in 2015, after receiving a grant from the Bank of Industry's Nollywood fund.

Maduegbuna wanted to expand Afrinolly into a full-service Nol-    93
lywood clearinghouse: equipment rental, soundstages, editing
bays, co-working facilities, classes, lectures, and meeting rooms.
(The post-production facilities would also be available for Nige-
rian companies shooting television commercials, most of which
were currently produced abroad). The office library was stocked
with books by CEOs about entrepreneurship and technology:
Richard Branson's *The Virgin Way*; Eric Schmidt's and Jared
Cohen's *The New Digital Age*; Cathie Black's *Basic Black*; *What
Every Angel Investor Wants You to Know* by Brian Cohen and John
Kador; *Lean In* by Sheryl Sandberg; *Start-up Nation: The Story of
Israel's Economic Miracle* by Dan Senor and Saul Singer.

At the time of my visit, the company's energy was focused
on a new venture, the Afrinolly Marketplace, which Maflueg-
buna hoped would be a major movie distribution platform for
Nigeria's 40 million smartphone users and the millions more
around Africa. On the Afrinolly Marketplace app, users would
be able to rent a movie for 100 naira using their airtime. (Phone
contracts are rare in Nigeria, and most mobile phone users buy
airtime via pay-as-you-go cards; using airtime to buy a movie
also meant that wary Nigerians or those outside the formal
banking system would not have to enter any credit card information.) He saw it as an anti-piracy platform—the movies would
not be permanently downloadable or shareable, or watched on
anything bigger than a mobile phone. Companies could include
Marketplace coupons as a promotional measure. The Marketplace would be accessible around Africa and Europe, with dif-
ferential pricing based on the purchasing power of a country's

population. At the time of my visit, Maduegbuna was trying to raise equity to fund the project.

I asked about data. Maduegbuna said, optimistically, that "the price has been crashing actually," also that the company had compressed the movie files. "A lot of people are now having access to wifi," he added. "Most people actually use their phone in the office or their friends' offices just to download it and watch it offline." But it was clear that data would be the biggest obstacle to the Marketplace's success, at least for now.

The story of Nollywood, however, is a story of an industry defined by its obstacles, and there is little doubt that Nolly-wood will adapt itself to a future model of distribution in ways that will likely be as unpredictable as the rise of the industry itself. Entrepreneurs like Maduegbuna and Njoku are trying to be there first, hoping that the technological shift from watching Nollywood movies on discs to watching them on phones will offer a chance to bring more profits back to the people who pro-duced the movies.

In late 2016, Nigeria overtook the UK in numbers of active sub-scribers to iRoko's Android app. Also that year, Njoku started what he called the "beyond data initiative." He opened 65 kiosks around Lagos where iRoko subscribers could pay for their sub-scriptions using cash or mobile money but also do data-free downloading of rented movies. (In Nigeria an iRoko subscrip-tion costs 500 naira a month, a third of the price of a movie ticket at the cinema but several times the price of a video CD at the market.) It's a canny initiative that may work, but it might also be the case that one day the same marketers who sell movies on disc will sell them via phone-to-phone transfer, or that friends will simply share movies among themselves. iRoko movies can only be shared between subscribers. In a market with a long tradition of circumventing digital rights management, with a distribution system that went global by ignoring copyright laws, wresting control of the profit chain will be a difficult, perhaps impossible goal.

## OJUJU (2014)
### DIRECTED BY C. J. OBASI

Recent Nollywood movies have dramatized the Ebola epidemic, the refugee crisis, and child marriage. *Ojuju* opens with shots of a riverbank under a bridge, the kind of urban shoreline where plastic refuse and tires accumulate and the murky water emits noxious smells. A title card comes up over the scene: "70 million Nigerians exist without safe access to safe drinking water," it reads. "The water pollution is caused by the discharge of untreated sewage, refuse, heavy metals, oil spills, pesticides, fertilizers, run-off from farms and other toxic chemicals into water bodies . . ."

The scene cuts to a labyrinthine slum of cinderblock houses. Refuse litters the streets. There is one way into this neighborhood and one way out, and only one source of water. The water, it turns out, carries a zombie virus, and soon a group of friends starts falling ill. The movie's male lead, played by Gabriel Afolayan, is named Romero, an homage to George Romero, who directed *Night of the Living Dead*. That movie used zombies to tell a story about race in America: A black man fights off a zombie invasion only to be shot by a white rabble who assumes he is a zombie. Here, the zombie appears in its Nigerian form, the *ojuju*, in a horror story about pollution in a country abounding with ecological disasters.

The flesh-eating monsters take over a neighborhood whose residents are used to having to fend for themselves. When their friends start getting bitey, they have no authorities to contact, and nowhere to flee.

"I'm telling you they're everywhere, it's like a movie," says one friend.

"Where are we going to go?" says Romero with a shrug. "This neighborhood is all we know."

There are no doctors to attend to the people falling ill. Those who can't afford medicine get an unsympathetic reception from the pharmacist (eventually the *ojuju* just eat him.) It's a battle between quick-witted young people with machetes and the slow-moving but tenacious *ojuju* horde, and even those who evade the undead eventually have to take a drink of water.

Like many horror movies, this one ends with the trope of the "final girl." Her name is Peju, and she is played by Omowunmi Dada. She sprints through the passages of the slum with her machete, following the painted arrows on the wall and the graffiti words "way out." Inside the slum, the *ojuju* have taken over. Outside it is Lagos as usual. She emerges from the passages of the neighborhood, blinking in the bright sunlight of an ordinary afternoon. She runs to a taxi, bleeding, and asks to be taken to the general hospital. "*Abeg, abeg,*" she says over and over, pidgin for "please." She is breathing heavily, and soon coughing blood. As the virus begins to take hold, the taxi driver apologizes for the delay: He has hit a traffic jam.

# Asaba

In Lagos, I was told many times over that to understand Nollywood, I had to go to Asaba.

Movies made in Asaba, the capital of Delta State, or Enugu,
another city in Eastern Nigeria, represented a different Nollywood from the more cinematic movies that have been produced in Lagos since the introduction of the multiplex in the
past decade. Nollywood is a unified industry, but there is a clear
delineation between a so-called "New Nollywood movie" and an
"Asaba movie."

The first difference is one of format: Movies made in Asaba
and Enugu tend to go straight to DVD or video disc and never
have cinema releases. They are sold exclusively in the market,
and while many have also found their way onto iRoko or You-
Tube, the marketers are not primarily concerned with digital or
cable distribution. Their business model depends primarily on
disc sales.

The second distinction is one of output: A New Nollywood producer might make one movie every year or two years.
An Asaba producer like Chidi Chijioke, Uche Nancy, or Ugezu
"Mr. Surplus" Ugezu will put out between ten and thirty movies
a year, with budgets that might be as low as five million naira
(about $25,000 in 2015) or as high as twenty million. The pay
is lower for actors and directors in Asaba, but the output of the
industry makes for steadier work. A successful Asaba-based
actor will make dozens of movies a year and hundreds over the
course of her career. While these movies do not have red carpet
premieres or hotel launches, the fame from working in one can
be much greater.

More than one actor told me that it was the work they did
in Asaba, even if it was just one movie, that earned them the
most recognition by strangers on the street. "The only Asaba
movie I've done got me more publicity than two years of the
world of Nollywood," said Ivie Okujaye, a young actor who has
scored leading roles in New Nollywood movies shot in Lagos.
After she made a movie in Asaba, she said, the market ladies
started to hail her when she went out shopping. (The market
woman is a literal but also proverbial figure in the Nigerian
national imagination who stands for a Nigerian everywoman, a
member of the urban working class.) As such, the Asaba/Lagos
divide is one of social class. As a poster on one online Nollywood forum put it, the reach of New Nollywood "seems to end
on the Island. . . . They are known mostly to Ajebutter crowds."
The Island is shorthand for the wealthiest neighborhoods of
Lagos; "ajebutter" is slang for "rich person." In contrast, the

commenter wrote, were "the normal Nollywood Asaba/Enugu movies that everyone knows." These were the movies of the people, the writer implied, "where the real money & fame are made. The movies might not be fantastic and all that, with crappy storylines, but that's the Nollywood that is known all over Africa and beyond."

I traveled to Asaba by air. The Niger River unfurled below, an opaque tan in color, its small islands dotted with white cows. The city formed a grid, where reddish-brown dirt side streets alternated with pavement thoroughfares. The Asaba airport was modern and calm. An Asaba-based production manager named Solomon Apete met me outside in an SUV. He wore a white t-shirt, black jeans, sneakers, and a big watch. He was a taciturn man of few words, but his silence carried authority, as I realized when we arrived on set.

Moviemaking in Asaba is done at a factory pace, and in his seven years in the industry Apete said he had produced more than four hundred movies. We drove to a rented house that was a permanent set for domestic dramas to see the movie Apete was producing that day, which as yet was untitled.

The roads of Asaba were less crowded than those of Lagos, and Apete said that one reason so much of the industry has left Lagos for smaller cities is the ease with which one can simply get from the airport to a set, something that in Lagos can take hours. The mechanical tricycles were painted blue here instead of yellow and carried optimistic slogans, like BETTER DAY

AHEAD, DETERMINATION LEADS TO SUCCESS, and BORN TO WIN. Billboards and posters advertised Pentecostal revivals: "Express Miracles presented by Jesus Church Bible Ministries, Inc." and "Jesus: the Game Changer: Three power-packed over-flooded services."

We arrived outside the concrete house where shooting was taking place. While we waited to enter without interrupting, Apete explained the different genres of movies that are made in Asaba, including "epics," which are historical dramas set in villages (there is a real village outside the city where many of these movies are shot) and where the actors wear traditional costume and "glamour" or "showcase" movies that show fashion trends, big houses, and nice cars. There are "royal" movies, where the plots feature tribal dynasties; Christian movies that feature moral lessons; and your basic action films, love stories, and comedies. The movie being shot today was what Apete characterized as a "family" movie. The term did not mean what it might mean in Hollywood, that it would be appealing to children. In Nollywood a family movie means that the drama is focused on the tribulations and struggles of a family over the course of generations.

The script for this particular movie was conceived by its director, Franklin Chinedum Nwoko, who described it as a "traditional story" about "family, emotion, greed, and lies." It is the story of a husband and wife who have had three daughters together. The husband is happy with the family, and does not mind the lack of male heirs, but his wife wants to give birth to a boy. She enters into a relationship with another man who has fathered seven male children in six years. Through their extra-marital relationship she conceives and gives birth to three sons. ("It is an African story," said Nwoko somewhat apologetically. "It's a man's world here.")

Her husband discovers the truth of his sons' paternity only on his deathbed. He is heartbroken, and lays a curse on the wife. "These children will kill you," he tells her. Years pass. The three boys grow wealthy and successful. Then, one by one, they go mad. The family loses everything. Only upon consultation with a man of god, who urges the mother to confess to her sins, is the curse of madness lifted—but it is too late for the mother, who dies.

We entered as the actors began rehearsing the moment in which one of the sons goes insane, just as he has been offered a major promotion. He sat at a table with the CEO of the company he worked for, along with his wife and a jealous rival. The table was set with porcelain dinner plates and unopened bottles of Moet. It was a bare bones production: two lights, one soundman with a boom mike, and a cameraman with a Canon E05 single-lens-reflex camera on a tripod with a digital recorder taped on top. A makeup artist stood ready to blot sweat. The crew of the movie numbered fewer than ten.

"My son," said the CEO, who was played by a gray-haired actor named Ofili Ugbo. "I have been impressed by your ability to move this company to greater heights." To get different angles on the scene, the cameraman lifted the camera off the tripod and knelt in various positions around the table, panning the hand-held camera back and forth.

"I hope by this time you're thinking of your master plan," said the CEO, raising his glass.

"Oh yes, sir," said the young man, played by a thirty-nine-year-old actor named Walter Anga. After toasting his promotion, the dinner party moved from the dining table to the living room. Anga, in character, suddenly let out an odd cackle. To bewildered looks by the other members of the cast, he started laughing maniacally, then threw the contents of his glass of champagne into the CEO's face as his wife frantically tried to restrain him.

In the next scene, a doctor conferred a grave diagnosis: "As it is, this case is beyond my control," he said, shaking his head. "It is obviously a psychiatric case. I'm sorry."

"My husband, my husband, my husband!" screamed the son's wife, collapsing to the floor in a paroxysm of grief.

An eighteen-hour day was not uncommon for Nollywood actors in Asaba, and after this scene concluded the cast and crew drove to the next location as night fell. When we arrived, crew members unloaded suitcases of props and light stands from a white-painted schoolbus that read "Nwafor Orizu College of Education, Nsugbe." Affixed to the hood were banners advertising the movies *Lion Hunters 1 & 2* and *Lion Hunters 3 & 4*, which showed collages of actors wielding bows and arrows, surrounded by roaring lion heads.

Franklin Nwoko set up a scene where the son angles for his promotion, sitting at a desk beneath a sign that said "Goodbye ignorance, you are dealing with a lawyer now." The painted walls of the room were dirty. The wires of the lights were plugged

directly into the sockets, and the lights flickered with the fluctu-
ations of the electricity, which was provided by a generator. It was
after 10:00 p.m. when Apete offered to drive me back to my hotel.
His crew would continue shooting until the movie wrapped.

The next day, Apete introduced me to a twenty-nine-year-old
actor named Daniel K. Daniel, one of the few Nollywood stars
whose career bridges Asaba and Lagos. DKD, as he is known,
had starred in New Nollywood movies like *A Soldier's Story*,
which at the time I met him was in its eighth week of cinema
release. He was in Asaba, however, for a movie that was more
representative of "Old Nollywood," a family story of a fortune
lost and gained via involvement with the occult, and the sub-
sequent rivalry between two brothers. "The masses don't want
to see you sipping champagne and Cristal and pizza or I don't
know," Daniel said. "For some reason they would rather see
someone in the village wearing clothes that they can identify
with, stuff like that."

The stories of Asaba were folkloric rather than topical,
and tended toward repetitive variation of well-worn themes:
a mother-in-law pressures a childless woman to get pregnant,
even if it means having an extramarital affair; a truck driver
crosses paths with a strange woman who is part of a deadly cult;
a friendship turns sour when one woman plots to seduce the
other's fiancé; a woman hits her head and has amnesia, forget-
ting her fiancé; a king demands to know which of his children
loves him best; a firstborn child or beloved wife is exchanged

for the base comforts of material wealth. The moviemakers' ability to recombine the same elements into original stories countless times over, writing scripts on their phones during power outages, reminded me of the thirty-one functions Vladimir Propp had once assigned to Russian fairytales. Many Nollywood movies ended with one of the tropes Propp described, namely: "recognition," "punishment," or "wedding."

The Asaba actors I spoke with often didn't bother to memorize lines. Scripts were rough outlines, and by memorizing the stories many of the actors could adopt archetypal roles and their speeches almost out of habit. I asked each actor I met about the previous movie he or she had worked on. Ofili Ugbo, who told me he averaged about four movies a month, had just wrapped one called *Painful Soul*, about a king who searches for a wife for his son while disguised as a beggar. Nosa Rex Okunzuwa, who said he loses count of how many movies he makes a year, had just finished one called *The Eagles*, about a group of soccer players who come to town for a testimonial match and "the girls get crazy." Solomon Apete described *Romantic Attraction*, the first movie he produced, about a little girl who sets her widowed father up with her schoolteacher.

Sitting in the back of Apete's SUV, I found pages of a discarded script stuffed in the back pocket of the front seat. The movie was the story of a nun who runs over the child of a blind beggar and loses her mind. The opening premise took a single page, as the beggars sit and sing for donations:

Chineye: *Mama, the money we have made today will not be enough for my school fee.*

Amarachi: *I know, by the time we finish passing this new song and get to the market with it, many people will give us money. Stand up, go and get the water.*

The script continued with stage directions: "There comes a car driving at high speed by the reverend sister," it said. After hitting Chinenye, the nun "carried the dead girl to the corner of the road and drove off weeping."

The nun ignores a dreamlike visitation from the Virgin Mary, who urges her to confess to the crime. Instead she goes mad. I only had a couple of pages of the script, and cannot say how it ended. I was sure a lover of Nollywood movies could probably predict the end, and would find satisfaction in doing so. I had watched enough movies to perhaps forecast the end myself—a confession, absolution by a priest, or perhaps an exorcism. The point of most Asaba movies was not to create something new, but to affirm a social order, its morality, its definitions of good and bad, and its ideals of success and failure. The real world might have unpredictable outcomes and rapid change, but in a movie from Asaba good and evil would be recognized, and rewarded or punished accordingly. The viewer could feel reassured of the rightness of the world.

## NKOLI NWA NSUKKA (2014)
### DIRECTED BY MAC COLLINS CHIDEBE ("MR. CHINA")

*Nkoli Nwa Nsukka* is an Igbo-language comedy about an irrepressible young woman from the region of Nsukka, in Eastern Nigeria. Nkoli lives with her mother and brother in a simple mud house with no electricity. She leads a local dance troupe that performs at weddings and other public events for money. She faces many hardships: Her mother is ill and the traditional healer will no longer extend them credit for herbal medicine. Nkoli's little brother wants to do an apprenticeship with a mechanic in the nearby city of Onitsha, but the cost to send him is too high. Nkoli loves her boyfriend, Magnus, but he has no job, and prospects for paid employment in their village are scarce. When her mother gets sicker, Nkoli is unable to pay the fee to hospitalize her and she dies. Then Magnus dumps her.

Brokenhearted and with nothing to lose, Nkoli makes her way to Onitsha herself, where she takes a job as a waiter. She is terrible at it—falling asleep on the job, dancing instead of serving food, yelling at a customer who dares to wink at her in front of his wife. She gets fired, but a rich man who noticed her dancing takes her in. Their relationship is murky: They call each other husband and wife but, as Nkoli's skeptical friend Asa points out, there has been no wedding. Still Nkoli now has a cell phone, a refrigerator, and lives in a mansion. Then Magnus shows up again, begging forgiveness.

The villager who goes to the city in search of a better life is a common theme in Nollywood movies, and in Nigerian life. Much

108    of the comedy in the movie is about Nkoli's provincialism—her
crass table manners, her tendency to fall asleep at her job, her
love for the ne'er-do-well Magnus. Her first encounters with
air conditioning, refrigeration, and a bridge spanning the Niger
River fill her with comic fear. This story proved so popular,
Nkoli such a loveable character, and the actor who played her,
Rachel Okonkwo, such a breakout star, that the plot of the original movie was extended for many more chapters. In *Nkoli Nwa
Nsukka* the gestures toward the struggles faced by most Nigerians are small but precise: A customer wants to order a cold
beer, but the ice blocks did not come in that day; Nkoli wants
news of her brother from Onitsha, but has to rely on words from
friends of friends; a woman dies because her family can't pay
the fee to hospitalize her (and nobody would criticize *Nkoli Nwa
Nsukka* for downplaying the Nigerian expression of mourning—
upon hearing of her mother's death Nkoli falls to her knees
screaming).

The comedic moments are also culturally specific: shouting
matches between customers and servers, passengers and
drivers, and boyfriends and girlfriends; Nkoli hijacking the
restaurant employees' morning prayer and turning it into an
extended sermon; the way that once she comes into money she
hails every street vendor from the window of the bus, buying
plantain chips, tapioca and coconut, bananas, apples, soda, peanuts, and disgusting the passenger sitting next to her by wolfing
them all down at once.

*Nkoli* is not a glamorous movie, but one where urbanity and
consumer culture are treated with suspicion. Villagers go to the

city and face moral corruption. They return with "swagger": polo shirts with popped collars, blue jeans, roller suitcases, watches, sunglasses, lipstick, headphones, loaves of white bread. The symbols of wealth are the same as in every Nollywood movie—mansions with columns, sport utility vehicles, and unopened bottles of champagne on the dinner tables—but here they are gently mocked. Nkoli makes endless class-based errors: refusing to take the phone her husband gives her out of the box because she doesn't want it to get dirty; marveling to see a television mounted on a wall and being terrified it will fall; not knowing how headphones work. When she puts on makeup she does so clownishly; her new outfits are worn slightly off-kilter. She adopts the bossiness expected of upper class Nigerians toward the people they pay to do things for them but she never loses her generosity. When a neighbor who wronged her is being dragged away for failing to pay a debt, Nkoli triumphantly bails him out. She acquires wealth without being spoiled by it. Her provincial cluelessness and bad taste are the signs of her authenticity and fundamental goodness.

The message is one of optimism and perseverance. Life in Nigeria is hard, and there is nothing to be done but continue living. "I'm tired of staying in this poor village," says Magnus to Nkoli. "What kind of life is this?"

"My love, let me tell you something," she responds with a frown. "You should stop thinking to avoid high blood pressure."

# Conclusion

When you leave Lagos, Nigeria, flying out to a different, calmer place (because there are more places in the world that are calmer than Lagos than there are places more hectic) it becomes a difficult city to recollect. I can remember certain aspects of it: the clusters of water plants in the lagoon as you drive over the Third Mainland Bridge; the energy-efficient lighting that gives the place its nighttime pallor (if there is light at all); the pervasive smell of camphor mothballs used as everything from insecticide in a restaurant booth to air freshener in a urinal. I can picture the lines of yellow minibuses, the hawkers with seasonal wares, and the elaborate Christmas decorations in the traffic circle by the Eko Hotel. I remember a motto painted outside a schoolyard "With Zeal the Best We Seek" and the teenagers on rollerblades who would skate through stalled traffic, holding on to the back of a transport van. (One rollerblader wore a t-shirt that said, in pidgin, "Don't Aske Me, Na God Win").

But the feeling of being in Nigeria is not captured in remembered visual details. Lagos has a mood, a sense of possibility, including that something very bad could happen at any moment. For a city so large there is little feeling of anonymity—neighbors know each other, strangers involve themselves in minor skirmishes, people start conversations from car windows and on the street. Many Nigerians have two or three phones to make up for the spotty coverage of individual networks, phones that ring all the time.

Sometimes, while waiting for an interview or sitting at a bar, a movie would be playing on the television, often a product of Hollywood. I would watch Daniel Craig falling into a whirlpool of water with a knife sticking out of his chest; or Tom Cruise writhing on a Japanese futon and yelling the word "sake"; or Mark Wahlberg on a mountain peak sighting a buck through a rifle scope; or Pierce Brosnan with a hardboiled dismissal ("You feel the need for a relationship? Get a dog.") When Nigerians talked about American blockbusters, they tended to mention how hard it was to relate to an airplane hijacking. Sitting in a bar in Lagos, sipping an Amstel Malta, I saw some of the wreckage of my own culture beaming around the world. These movies, silly when I watched them at home, were sillier than ever outside of America.

Today the monocultural human in almost any country in the world wears a t-shirt, jeans, and flip-flops, sits in a stackable white plastic bar chair under a low-wattage fluorescent light, drinks a sweetened carbonated beverage, and sends a text message while watching the local franchise of *The Voice* or *Big Brother*. Humanity now has a common visual vernacular: in Hollywood, Bollywood, Nollywood, Korean drama, and the Latin American telenovela the symbols of material wealth are imported bottles of liquor, big watches, sleek cars, and carefully styled hair. Maids come from villages to big cities and are pure of heart. Gangsters have guns, bricks of powdered drug shipments, and stacks of cash. Villains wear bold colors; heroines pastels. The soundtracks are composed on keyboard synths and the credit sequences made using software templates. But globalization is no longer necessarily synonymous with cultural imperialism, or with the domination of a single country's entertainment output. There is a joke in the movie *Taxi Driver*, when Adigun learns his father named his taxi "Tom Cruise": "Tom Cruise," says Adigun. "Isn't he an Indian actor?"

Globalization did not produce a single cultural capital, but several of them. Yet until the creation of the Nigerian video movie industry, also known as Nollywood, none of this globalized content addressed the sub-Saharan African experience.

The first wave of post-independent African cinema often had an ideological mission: to correct the misrepresentation of African history and African life and to confront the legacy of imperialism; to affirm the value of specific African cultures, heritages, and identities. But as the Cameroonian philosopher Achille Mbembe has written, "Because the time we live in is fundamentally fractured, the very project of an essentialist or sacrificial recovery of the self is, by definition, doomed. Only the disparate, and often intersecting, practices through which Africans *stylize* their conduct and life can account for the thickness of which the African present is made." Nollywood marks this phase of self-writing, where the assertion of Nigerian identity is not conducted in opposition to the forces of globalization and multiculturalism, but within them. Nollywood movies not only address the specificities of the Nigerian experience: They project an African identity outward into the globalized flow of popular culture, that transcendent sphere from which a teenager in Atlanta learns Nigerian pidgin slang, or a movie director in Lagos takes a cue from Scorsese.

Nigerian movies can be melodramatic, filled with cliché, badly paced, and overly sentimental. Once, while on a shoot for a movie that might be called "the New New Nollywood"—a generation of young directors who are making what would, in a country with more movie theaters, be called art-house movies—I listened as the young crew sat around remembering the worst Nollywood movies they had ever seen: a ghost story where the ghost has to try and cross the street without getting hit by a car ("She was supposed to be a wraith!"); a movie that was described only as the "Hausa *Titanic*;" another called *Spider Girl* where the heroine wears a packaged Spider-Man Halloween costume and launches into the air with the electronic "woosh" sound that typically accompanied the apparition of ghosts in old Nollywood movies.

"Was it good?"

"No, it was not. It was awful."

(I later looked up *Spider Girl*, which had a respectable 70,000 views on YouTube. Most of the comments made use of the laughing-until-crying emoji.)

The movie being shot that December day was an action story called *Slow Country*, directed by an up-and-coming film-maker named Eric Aghimien who was hoping for (and ultimately achieved) a cinema release. The shoot was at the Owode Onirin auto parts market on the outskirts of Lagos, near a neighbor-hood known simply as Mile 12. During the week, I was told, this market would be packed, and was known to be a rough scene with, said a crew member, "lots of pushing and shoving." But now the market was as quiet as Wall Street on a Sunday, a grave-yard of dead cars, the carcasses of Range Rovers and Toyotas organized into stacks of fenders, grills, and tires. The sky was cloudless and the light gold in the late afternoon light. The air smelled faintly of raw sewage from the open gutters. The quiet was broken only by the paces of the occasional security guards, who patrolled the grounds with machetes or leather whips.

*Slow Country* was an action movie, and all the Tony Mon-tana details were in order—fake guns, white powders, thug-gish bodyguards, a prostitute with a heart of gold. The team was shooting a getaway scene using a rusted blue Nissan Sunny with a manual transmission that had to be pushed to get into gear. As usual, interference from the outside world kept delaying the shoot: a broken-down car in the path of the Nissan that the actors had to roll out of the way; a group of Liberians who were towing in a wreck and making too much noise. The sun had started to get low in the sky.

Between shots, I started chatting with a crew member who was also standing around watching. He turned out to be a spe-cial effects man, who introduced himself as Hakeem "Effect"

Onilogbo. I asked him how he got into the business. He said he was self-taught. He used to be a sign-painter, but when the Lagos state government outlawed billboards in 2006 he was put out of work. He had trouble finding a new profession that suited his artistic temperament.

"I'm a melancholy," he said. "I have a lot of things in me."

He decided to learn how to do movie makeup. "I put in for acting, but I don't go in with the crowd," he said. "I wanted to do something special, so that's when I ventured into special effects."

The materials used by professional effects artists were hard to get in Nigeria, so he began by improvising, mostly using "different African foods." Today he uses latex. His reputation grew until now, at thirty-seven, he was one of the most sought after FX experts in the industry. He worked with his sister, who was also on set, ready to craft gunshot wounds.

We stood and watched the action, which had resumed. Aghimien, the director, was a hipsterish thirty-something with a short afro and black-framed glasses. He crawled into the back of the car to get sound as the actors drove.

"Director you are wasting my time, it is six o'clock oh," said the production manager, who was getting anxious. "Let's do this, let's do this, let's do this. Roll, roll, roll." The light faded and the shooting wrapped.

From a slow-moving traffic jam on the way back to the center of the city I peered out at the edges of the vast Mile 12 food market in the growing darkness. Women sold peeled oranges, hot peppers, and sachets of laundry detergent under battery-powered lights.

116    A father and a toddler walked along the road in matching out-
       fits. A herd of goats drank water by the side of the road. From
       inside a van stuck in traffic a church group clapped and sang. It
       was all this life that Nollywood could capture, and beam back
       out to the world.

# Acknowledgments

I want to thank everyone who helped me in Nigeria, especially Uzodinma Iweala, for hosting me, and Solomon Iseoluwa and his deputy Bisi for keeping us safe on the roads of Lagos. Thank you also to everyone who generously shared their knowledge about Nollywood: Kemi Adesoye, Eric Aghimien, Ijeoma Grace Agu, Oris Aigbokhaevbolo, Jerry Amilo, Walter Anga, Jahman Anikulapo, Tunde Apalowo, Solomon Apete, Bemigho Awala, Tunde Babalola, Moses Babatope, Seyi Babatope, Ishaya Bako, Ego Boyo, Daniel K. Daniel, Rita Dominic, Desmond Elliot, Badaiki "Shaggy" Erom, Shaibu Husseini, Amara Iwuala, Tunde Kelani, Chike Maduegbuna, Obi Madubogwu, Wangi Mba-Uzoukwu, Kene Mkparu, Ben Murray-Bruce, Jason Njoku, Sambasa Nzeribe, Femi Odugbemi, Okey Ogunjiofor, Izu Ojukwu, Franklin Okoro, Gabriel "Gabosky" Okoye, Ivie Okujaye, Nosa Rex Okunzuwa, Mildred Okwo, Francis Onwochei, Daniel Oriahi, Lucky Oseghale, Taiwo Samuel, Walter Taylaur, Tope Tedela, Chief Philip Udi, Ofili Ugbo, and Christopher Vourlias.

SIGNAL AND NOISE
*Media, Infrastructure, and Urban Culture in Nigeria* (Duke University Press, 2008). By Brian Larkin. This academic survey of the media in Nigeria includes a chapter on the infrastructure of video piracy.

NOLLYWOOD
*The Video Phenomenon in Nigeria* (Indiana University Press, 2009). Edited by Pierre Barrot. Translated from the French by Lynn Taylor from the 2005 original, this collection of essays is divided into two parts. The first documents Nollywood in Nigeria, with chapters on censorship, distribution, and digital technology; the second is about Nollywood's impact around Africa. Contributors include Nollywood directors Don Pedro Obaseki and Tunde Kelani, as well as other industry experts.

MOVIEDOM, THE NOLLYWOOD NARRATIVES
*Clips on the Pioneers* (All Media International, 2010). By Shaibu Husseini. This book by a movie critic for *The Guardian* newspaper of Nigeria has short profiles of important industry figures.

NOLLYWOOD TILL NOVEMBER
*Memoirs of a Nollywood Insider* (AuthorHouse, 2012). By Charles Novia. This memoir by a Nollywood director who began directing in 2000 is an opinionated and dishy book about the end-to-end process of making, marketing, and distributing movies in Lagos.

GLOBAL NOLLYWOOD
*The Transnational Dimensions of an African Video Film Industry* (Indiana University Press, 2013). Edited by Matthias Krings and Onookome Okome. A collection of fifteen essays about the global reception of Nollywood.

NOLLYWOOD STARS
*Media and Migration in West Africa and the Diaspora* (Indiana University Press, 2015). By Noah Tsika. An academic analysis of Nollywood's star system that examines the nuances of Nigerian celebrity culture.

120    NOLLYWOOD
THE CREATION OF NIGERIAN FILM GENRES (UNIVERSITY OF CHICAGO PRESS, 2016)
By Jonathan Haynes. Written by one of the foremost scholars of Nollywood in America, this book compiles more than two decades of research
by Haynes. At more than four hundred pages, it is the most comprehensive history of Nollywood, with information about everything from the
influence of Yoruba theater traditions to specifics about the social, political, and economic contexts that inform the tropes of Nigerian movies.
Organized by genre rather than chronologically, the book also includes
summaries of many of the most important movies in Nollywood history
and profiles of major directors.

NOLLYWOOD CENTRAL (PALGRAVE, 2016)
By Jade L. Miller. This is a brisk and comprehensive survey of the industry,
with chapters on Nollywood's history and its business practices, audiences,
relationship to the Nigerian government, and global reach. Miller pays particular attention to the "alternative media networks" by which Nollywood
achieved global distribution outside of dominant channels of capital.

"THE NETFLIX OF AFRICA DOESN'T NEED HOLLYWOOD TO WIN"
*BloombergBusinessWeek*, February 22, 2016 (https://www.bloomberg.com/
news/features/2016-02-22/the-netflix-of-africa-doesn-t-need-holly-
wood-to-win). By Alexis Okeowo. A magazine profile of Jason Njoku and
iRoko TV.

"A SCORSESE IN LAGOS"
*The New York Times*, February 23, 2012 (http://wwwnytimes.
com/2012/02/26/magazine/nollywood-movies.html). By Andrew Rice. A
magazine-length overview of Nollywood with a focus on New Nollywood
director Kunle Afolayan.

NOTES

**29  it was in part the decline:**
*Nollywood: The Video Phenomenon in Nigeria*, edited by Pierre Barrot, p. 40

**32  The numbers are still small:**
"'Wedding Party' Fuels Record Nigerian Box Office Despite Ailing Economy," by Christopher Vourlias, *Variety*, February 3, 2017. http://variety.com/2017/film/global/wedding-party-fuels-record-nigerian-box-office-despite-ailing-economy-1201977878/

**33  one prominent Nollywood director: "Nollywood Director to Genevieve Nnaji:** 'Instead of Blasting Nollywood, Come and Improve Nollywood'" *Pulse*, July 3, 2014. http://www.pulse.ng/gist/nollywood-director-to-genevieve-nnaji-instead-of-blasting-nollywood-come-and-improve-nollywood-id2960209.html

**34  *Road to Yesterday*:** The movie is currently available for streaming in the United States on Netflix.

**45  Jos had been bombed by Boko Haram a few months before:**
"Scores killed as church, mosques are targeted in Nigeria," CNN, July 6, 2015 http://www.cnn.com/2015/07/06/africa/nigeria-violence/index.html

**45  As Chinua Achebe once wrote:** *The Trouble with Nigeria* (Heinemann, 1983) by Chinua Achebe, p. 10.

**45  We are somewhere:** "Escaped Lion from Jos Wildlife Park Killed" *The Guardian*, December 3, 2015, by Isa Abdulsalami Ahovi https://t.guardian.ng/news/escaped-lion-from-jos-wildlife-park-killed/

**46  This evasion caused lively debate:** "Who Released, Killed, and Ate Our Lion?" *Express*, December 11, 2015, by Reuben Abati. http://expressng.com/2015/12/reuben-abati-who-released-killed-and-ate-our-lion/

**48  Jews of West Africa:** "Breakup in Nigeria," *The Nation*, May 30, 1967, by Stanley Meisler.

**48  The Facebook Page of Brother Kenneth Nnebue Film Evangelism:** https://www.facebook.com/nekvideolinks/

**49  In 2015 Nnebue sold the rights:** "Awaiting Second Coming of Living in Bondage," *The Guardian Sunday Magazine*, October 31, 2015, by Chuks Nwanne. https://guardian.ng/sunday-magazine/awaiting-second-coming-of-living-in-bondage/

**51  a temporary husband:** http://www.historyandwomen.com/2010/08/amina-of-zaria.html

**60  More than 375,000 Nigerians:** "The Nigerian Diaspora in the United States," Migration Policy Institute, June 2015. http://www.migrationpolicy.org/research/select-diaspora-populations-united-states

**63  Nigerian workers painted:** One irony of privatization has been that infrastructure projects in Africa are often contracted to state-owned companies from India and

122   China. The Badagry Expansion is overseen by the China Civil Engineering Construction Corporation. "We'll Complete Lagos-Badagry Expressway by 2019" *Vanguard*, November 3, 2016. http://www.vanguardngr.com/2016/11/well-complete-lagos-badagry-expressway-expansion-2019-ambode/

66   **an estimated 1.2 million subscribers in Nigeria:** "Entertainment and Media Outlook: 2015–2019, South Africa-Nigeria-Kenya" PriceWaterhouseCoopers, September 2016. https://www.pwc.co.za/en/assets/pdf/entertainment-and-media-outlook-2015-2019.pdf

69   **A 2009 *New York Times* article:** "The Other Tinseltown," *New York Times*, February 20, 2009, by Paul Berger. http://www.nytimes.com/2009/02/22/nyregion/thecity/22noll.html

70   **the Brooklyn District Attorney's office:** "Pirated Films from Nigeria Are Seized in Brooklyn," *New York Times*, November 4, 2010, by Kareem Fahim. http://www.nytimes.com/2010/11/05/nyregion/05nollywood.html

70   **Genevieve Nnaji told the Toronto International Film Festival:** "In Conversation with Genevieve Nnaji and Kunle Afolayan," Toronto International Film Festival, September 12, 2016. The discussion can be watched online at https://www.youtube.com/watch?v=HdMhujWo-nA

71   **I soon learned that *October 1*:** "Pirated copies of October 1 film now released, please don't buy," *Pulse*, April 13, 2015, by Chidumga Izuzu. http://www.pulse.ng/movies/kunle-afolayan-pirated-copies-of-october-1-film-now-released-please-dont-buy-id3650145.html

71   **Piracy alarm:** Notice posted on Lancelot Imasuen's Instagram feed. https://www.instagram.com/p/BUAQH3vltBu/?taken-by=lancelotimasuen

72   **for which she served as brand ambassador:** "Photos from Rachael Okonkwo's (Nkoli Nwa Nsukka) Annual Children's Easter carnival 2017." http://www.lindaikejisblog.com/2017/04/photos-from-rachael-okonkwos-nkoli-nwa.html

73   **Some had organized street protests:** "Piracy: Nollywood Producers, Actors Protest to Fashola's office" *The Independent*, April 21, 2015. http://independent.ng/piracy-nollywood-producers-actors-protest-fasholas-office/

73   **I started arresting them:** "Top Filmmaker, Gabosky, Exposes Pirates in Nollywood," Yes! International Magazine, July 18, 2016. http://theyesng.com/top-film-maker-gabosky-exposes-pirates-in-nollywood/

80   **The entry to the petrol depots in Apapa:** "Unlocking the Apapa Traffic Gridlock" *The Nation*, July 7, 2015, by Adeyinka Aderibigbe and Miriam Ekene-Okoro. http://thenationonlineng.net/unlocking-the-apapa-traffic-gridlock/

80   **The actual order of event:** "In the Encounter, Fiction Meets Reality," *This Day*, November 22, 2015, by Yinka Olatunbosun. http://allafrica.com/stories/20151 1231632.html

88   **By 2016, this business, called iRoko:** "From 'Netflix of Africa' to 'Nollywood' Producer," *Financial Times*, July 31, 2016, by Maggie Fick https://www.ft.com/ content/d98743b4-4dd0-11e6- 88c5-db83e98a590a and "The Netflix of Africa Doesn't Need Hollywood to Win," *Bloomberg Businessweek*, February 22, 2016, by Alexis Okeowo. https://www .bloomberg.com/news/features/ 2016-02-22/the-netflix-of-africa- doesn-t-need-hollywood-to-win

94   **In late 2016:** "Beyond Data," Just Me [personal blog of Jason Njoku], January 9, 2017. https:// jason.com.ng/beyond-data-9e60e- b136c2b

99   **As a poster on one online Nollywood forum put it:** "New Cinema Nollywood Versus Asaba Nollywood," Nairaland discussion thread, January 27, 2016. http://www .nairaland.com/2895821/new- cinema-nollywood-versus-asaba

112   **As the Cameroonian philosopher Achille Mbembe:** "African Modes of Self-Writing," *Public Culture*, Volume 1, Number 1, Winter 2002, by Achille Mbembe, translated by Steven Rendall, p. 272.